THE FINE ART OF PUBLIC WORSHIP

THE
FINE ART
OF
PUBLIC WORSHIP

ANDREW W BLACKWOOD
Professor of Homiletics
THE THEOLOGICAL SEMINARY
Princeton, New Jersey

ABINGDON PRESS
New York • *Nashville*

THE FINE ART OF PUBLIC WORSHIP

Copyright MCMXXXIX by Whitmore & Smith

L

SET UP, PRINTED, AND BOUND BY THE
PARTHENON PRESS, AT NASHVILLE,
TENNESSEE, UNITED STATES OF AMERICA

0072967

DEDICATED

TO THE

WESTMINSTER

CHOIR COLLEGE

FOREWORD

The purpose of this book is practical. It grows out of a conviction, an ideal, and an experience.

The conviction is that the time has come for a revival of public worship as the finest of the fine arts. If preaching is a fine art, as many of us believe, public worship should be finer, as the whole should be better than any of the parts. While there is a call for strong preaching, there is even greater need for uplifting worship. Any man whose work takes him from one church to another can testify that he brings away something good from almost every sermon, but that he seldom enjoys a feeling of uplift during other parts of public worship, notably the prayers. In many a parish, such a friendly observer finds that the young people are not enthusiastic about the church. They are even more critical of the music and the prayers than of the preaching. In such a parish, there should be a revival of public worship. Such a revival begins with the pastor.

The ideal is that every minister should be a master of this fine art. One of many signs that the revival of public worship may come in fullness ere long is that the local pastor is becoming dissatisfied with his ways of leading. The temptation is to start the movement toward better things by tinkering with the order of service, forgetting that it makes little difference how one arranges unworthy hymns, readings, and prayers.

Before one tries to improve the order of service, would it not be wise to consider the meaning and the glory of public worship? To do that, one turns to the Bible, the history of the Church, and the findings of present-day ministers who excel in this art. After such a course, one should have set up certain ideal standards, to guide and restrain in making one's plans. Such is the practical aim in writing the present book.

The experience back of the book is of one who was for years a busy pastor, serving in fields of various sorts, but not among the very rich. While in more recent years the Lord has honored me by permitting me to become a teacher of young ministers, I am still at heart a pastor. I think of the pastor's work as the choicest privilege which he bestows upon any man in our modern world, excepting only the foreign missionary. On the basis of my own experiences, and intimate contacts with hundreds of young ministers whom I have taught, as well as with many others who are older, I have tried to adapt lofty ideals to meet the needs of the local parish, which may not be large. If I have covered a good deal of ground, one reason is because many a pastor is able to purchase only one book in this field. That one book should deal with the subject as a whole.

Here at Princeton, for a number of years, I have taught a class in worship at the Seminary, and another at the Westminster Choir College. One reason why I hope to see a revival of public worship as a fine art is because I believe in these young people who are going out to be the leaders of worship in many a local sanctuary. With them I have tried to share my vision of a better day, and to them I am grateful for much that they have taught me. One lesson which they have helped me to learn is that such a book as this should deal with the troublesome question, "How?" May the Lord bless the book, and use it as a means of helping many a busy pastor to find the answer to this ever-present question.

                                        ANDREW W. BLACKWOOD

The Theological Seminary
Princeton, New Jersey.

CONTENTS

CHAPTER I

THE FINE ART AND THE ARTIST

*I*N what sense is public worship a fine art? According to one use of the term, the fine arts include music and architecture, poetry and the drama, as well as two or three others which do not concern us now. There is an obvious connection between worship and music, as between worship and architecture. Though it is not so obvious, there is a real connection between worship and poetry, as in the use of hymns and psalms, and in the general sense of rhythm. Some wise men even think of public worship, notably the Lord's Supper, in terms of sacred drama.[1] But this is not what one has in mind when one speaks of worship as a fine art.

In the everyday use of the word, an art refers to skill in making certain actions, as in playing the pipe organ; and in using certain means to attain desired ends, as in writing a hymn for use at the dedication of a church. Some of our modern arts, such as teaching or nursing, are extremely practical; they appeal to the sons and daughters of Martha. Other arts, such as music, are chiefly aesthetic; when they are true to their God-given purpose, they appeal to the sons and daughters of Mary. These fine arts

[1] *Art and Religion,* Yale Press, 1921, and *Modern Worship,* Yale Press, 1927, both by Van Ogden Vogt.

13

belong in the realm of beauty; their appeal is largely to the imagination. It should be clear, therefore, that public worship is closer to the fine arts than to the practical. At least among Christians, public worship seems to be the best of all the fine arts.

On the basis of the materials with which they deal, and the human needs to which they minister, the practical arts seem to be good; the fine arts, better; and public worship, best of all. Here the subject matter is the truth concerning the ways of God in his dealings with men, supremely in Christ; the appeal is to the souls of the persons whom he is calling to become his children, as well as his agents in advancing his kingdom throughout the world. Except in the realm of religious poetry, such as that of Dante and Milton, and in the sphere of religious music, such as that of Bach and Handel, where is the artist who uses words and melodies for such heavenly purposes as we ministers use them whenever we lead in the public worship of God?

So let us think about the meaning of public worship as a fine art, and then about the leader as an artist second to none among men. If for a while we are concerned chiefly with ideals, later we shall see how they work in the actual conduct of public worship today.

THE MEANING OF PUBLIC WORSHIP

Worship is man's response to God's revelation of himself. In a high sense worship includes both the revelation and the response, but in this book we are concerned chiefly with the response. Two or three times a week the children of God should worship him in his house, publicly. Three times daily the members of every Christian family should give thanks to God before they eat together, and if possible they should tarry after both the morning and the evening meal to worship together, socially. Night and morning, as well as at other times of need or desire, every child of God should read the Bible and pray, secretly. Such is the Christian ideal of worship, public, social, and private. With us now, the concern is about public worship. It differs from family prayers or private devotions much as the assembled congregation differs from the family group or the individual Christian.

During much of the time, we shall think about public worship as it concerns one man among many. Taking one who is typical of our religion at its best, we shall watch him as he worships among his own people, and note how he responds to God's revelation of himself. As such an object lesson, we may think of young Isaiah in the temple. Forgetting that he was to become the most powerful of ancient preachers, we shall take his experience as our approach to that of the man in the pew today. While there is already too much individualism in our thoughts about public worship, which is the corporate response of God's people, we can see the facts more clearly if we look at them as they concern this one case. Such an approach is practical, rather than philosophical.[2]

In the hour of worship, the man in the pew should re-

<hr>

[2] Cf. *Christian Worship*, ed. by Nathaniel Micklem, Oxford Press, 1936, pp. 1-18.

should respond in 4 ways

spond to God's revelation of himself much as Isaiah did;[3] that is, in four different ways, and almost always in the same order. First, there ought to be the feeling of awe and wonder in the presence of the holy God. "Holy, holy, holy!" While the record does not say so, it is clear that the young man made in his heart the right response to what he saw and heard about the glory of God. Second, there is the confession of sins, both personal and social. Third, there is the experience of God's cleansing and redeeming grace. Here again, the worshiper is passive, except as by faith he gladly accepts what the Lord graciously bestows. Fourth, there is the dedication of heart and life to God for service among men. As we learn from the latter part of this golden chapter, the service would lead to hardship, danger, and apparent failure.

Every such experience is extremely personal. In the hour of public worship, the layman becomes conscious of three or four different persons, or groups of persons. First of all, and most important, he should think of God, as the Holy One, the Merciful Father, tender to sympathize and mighty to save. Second, the worshiper should think of himself, as he is in the eyes of God. In actual experience, the average man thinks about himself before he thinks about God; but we are now concerned with the ideal. Third, he thinks about the people near him in church, and about others like them, all of whom need God's redeeming grace. Fourth, at the time he may

[3] Isa. 6:1-8.

16

or may not be thinking much about those who lead in song and in prayer, but in later reflection he gives the leaders their place, which may be last on the list. What an ideal!

This way of thinking about the consciousness of the man in the pew leads to a vital question, about the proper balance between the objective and the subjective. The books about the psychology of Christian experience keep saying that the worship of the typical Protestant church-goer in the United States is largely subjective, whereas it ought to be chiefly objective.[4] What the writers mean is that the average man in the pew seems to direct his attention primarily to himself and his needs, whereas he should turn his mind and heart toward God, desiring to come into closer touch with him, to become right with him, and perhaps to make some desired effect upon him. In other words, the wrong way to worship is to strive to get; the right way is to wish to give. In subjective worship, the man in the pew thinks about himself, his feelings, his needs, and his desires. For example, think of the difference between the man who sings from the heart, "Holy, holy, holy," and the one who sings with equal earnestness, "O that will be, glory for me, glory for me, glory for me."

It is scarcely fair, however, to paint such a picture solely in black and white. As an example of subjective worship in one of its more pleasing forms, take a Christian En-

---

[4] E.g., *The Religious Consciousness*, by James B. Pratt, Macmillan, 1928, chap. xiv.

17

deavor topic suggested a number of years ago. "What Do We Get from Worship?" In many a society, that may have been the first time that the young folk ever thought much about the meaning of public worship. If the discussion had brought out the unifying theology which our Lord taught the woman at the well,[5] they might have received an inspiration for life. But if one may judge from some of the "helps," showing the leader how to plan "a bright, happy service, with no long, painful pauses," the singing, the speaking, and the praying were almost wholly introspective. If so, were the young people at fault? How could they have told one another what they did not know, or expressed what they had not experienced? Such young folk need expert leadership.

Among the leaders in the various Protestant churches today, there is a growing desire for more of the objective element in public worship. Theoretically, it would be possible to move so far in that direction as to run the risk of losing the very man whom we are anxious to help. Even in the holiest hour, the man in the pew does not cease to be human, with all sorts of human interests and desires. If our worship should become almost wholly objective, it might seem to such a man as cold as Durham Cathedral on a cloudy day in December. For instance, only the exceptional layman feels any quickening of the pulse when he sings Joseph Addison's purely objective hymn, "The spacious firmament on high," set to Haydn's stately music, "Creation." While there should be a place

[5] John 4:19-24.

18

for such a purely objective hymn, at least once in a while, there is need also of others more largely subjective. The same principle applies to our public prayers. How, then, can we secure the proper balance?

If objective worship is likely to seem cold, subjective worship is almost sure to be weak. When Woodrow Wilson was here at Princeton, he aroused a temporary tempest among certain Bible school teachers by telling them to have nothing to do with such songs as "Beautiful isle of somewhere," a song in which there is little suggestion of anything divine. In the University one of his young kinsmen was a member of the chapel choir, which loved to sing the anthem based on the first part of the twenty-seventh psalm, "The Lord is my light and my salvation; whom shall I fear?" A few years later, when this young man found himself in a zero hour at the front in France, the words of the anthem came into his heart and enabled him to conquer his fears. When such a young man's heart is crying out for God, he should be able to look higher than to a beautiful island, which seems to be nowhere. Doubtless such a statement is extreme. If so, where is the golden mean?

(In the hour of worship, there should be a blending of the objective and the subjective, with the objective prevailing, especially in the early part of the service.) Such is the emphasis in the opening words of the Shorter Catechism, "Man's chief end is to glorify God, and to enjoy him forever." Still more beautiful is the blending of the two elements in Charles Wesley's hymn, "Love di-

19

vine, all loves excelling." Like all true religion, this song begins with the truth about God in Christ, and leads up to the ideal relation between the worshiper and God. The closing line, "Lost in wonder, love, and praise," is superb. It might well be put in some attractive form and hung over the minister's study table, to guide him in planning for every hour of worship.

Whenever we mortals worship God, the determining factor is his character. Sometimes we think more about matters of time and place, rites and ceremonies, than we think about him. With the woman at the well, to whom the Lord Jesus explained the meaning of public worship, we need to learn that where anyone has the will to worship God, he is waiting to show that person how; and that where the will to worship is not present, all our human devices are but as sounding brass and tinkling cymbal. "God is a Spirit: and they that worship him must worship him in spirit and in truth"; that is, our worship must be sincere, and it must be real. Here, then, should be our emphasis, "Worship Him!"

THE LEADER OF PUBLIC WORSHIP

In every hour of public worship, there should be a leader who is trained. In the quietness of his room, every Christian should be able to worship God acceptably. At the family altar, and in the midweek meeting, the prayers of an untutored man are often uplifting. But when scores or hundreds of people come together to worship God in his house, they should have expert leadership.

Later we shall think about the leaders of the music; here we are concerned with the minister as the leader of the entire service What, then, should be his practical philosophy concerning this vital part of his life work?

Many a thoughtful man of God looks upon himself in public worship as primarily a prophet. This word prophet literally means one who speaks for another. That Other for whom the present-day prophet speaks is God. As in the preaching of Isaiah or Micah, the message may be about the past or the future; but it is more likely to be about the present, on the basis of the past and in the light of the future. Whatever the element of time, the heart of the message has to do with God. First in the reading from the Scriptures, and then in the preaching of the Gospel, the constant endeavor is to make the truth as it is in God, or in Christ, both clear and luminous. While the truth itself may be as old as time, the prophet of God knows how to make it seem as new as the sunlight which streams through the stained glass windows.

It would be impossible to overemphasize the importance of the minister's work as a prophet. This is one of the most characteristic notes in the teachings of Karl Barth.[6] He insists that God makes himself known today supremely in Christ, that he does so through the Scriptures, and that his favorite method of making known the Christ who speaks in the Scriptures is through preaching. Preaching, then, is present-day revelation. Barth also insists that, whatever the means of revelation, its value

[6] *The Word of God and the Word of Man,* Pilgrim Press, 1928, pp. 186 ff.

21

for any one person depends upon his acceptance and his response. Thus far, many of us can go with Barth in his emphasis upon the minister as a prophet.

There is among Protestants even more need for emphasis upon the minister as a priest. If it is the prophet's mission to speak for God to men, it is the priest's privilege to speak for men to God. As in the case of Jeremiah or Ezekiel, the man of God today can be both a prophet and a priest. In a high sense, according to the New Testament, every Christian is a priest, with direct and immediate access to the mercy seat. But when the people come together for public worship, they need someone to represent them before God, and that is what is meant by the priestly work of the minister. Just as the father speaks for the household at family prayers, so does the pastor speak for the entire congregation in their corporate prayers to God. Whether or not we use the word priest, we should cherish the truth for which the word stands. Why quarrel about words?

The word leader is more likely to be popular. People who would not understand the minister if he spoke of himself as a prophet, and who would object if he referred to himself as a priest, are accustomed to think of him as their leader in worship. The figure seems to be that of a shepherd leading his flock, or perhaps a musician such as Stokowski leading the Philadelphia Symphony Orchestra. As the spirit of the true leader in worship is that of persuasiveness rather than force, so is that of the shepherd and of the orchestral leader, though either of them has practically absolute power over those that he is leading. So in public worship the ideal leader would be the one whom the people would follow without thinking that they were being led.

Here, then, is the prophet, the priest, the leader. While these distinctions should be clear to the minister, it is much more important for him to remember his controlling purpose in the conduct of public worship. Here as elsewhere, his chief desire is to bring the people, one by one, into right relations with God, and then into right relations with everyone else, with a new determination to do God's holy will on earth as it is done in heaven. Is there any undertaking which is more difficult and more delicate than that of the leader?

The difficulty in the leadership of public worship is largely threefold. First is the difficulty of making God seem real. In leading men and women who have been trained in school to think psychologically or scientifically —any way rather than in terms of God and the soul—how can one find words to make the supreme truths appear to be real and practical? Though many a modern man or woman is dissatisfied with the husks which the world has to offer, and is wistfully groping after something to satisfy the hunger of the heart, it is necessary to appeal to such a person on the present level of thought and feeling, and then gradually lead up to the place where God will become the most real fact in life. Of course that depends upon the work of the Holy Spirit in regeneration, but

23

here we are thinking about the human side of leadership towards God.

A second difficulty is that of making public worship interesting. What is sure to be interesting to the man whom we are trying to lead? According to the late editor of the *American Magazine,* who made it the most popular journal of its kind, the average man is more concerned about himself than about all things else. While such selfishness lies close to the roots of sin, the question remains, how can we appeal to such a man without robbing Christian worship of its distinctive glory? Obviously, the man needs to have a personal experience of Christ's redeeming and transforming grace. But largely for that very reason, the leader should make the hour of public worship the most interesting experience of the entire week.

A third difficulty is that of making every part of the hour distinctly Christian. This difficulty is really only a combination of the other two; for if one makes every part center in Christ, each part will be full of reality as it is in God, and at the same time warm with human interest. In Christ, God and man find each other. The secret of such Christ-centered leadership is to have a vital experience of one's own, and to renew it from day to day. Otherwise, how could one lead others further into the holy mount than one has ever gone? However, the right sort of leader finds no insuperable difficulty in bringing Christ to his friends, and in bringing his friends into the presence of Christ. Here again, the power is in the Holy

Spirit, who is waiting to bless a man's leadership. Instead of thinking about the difficulties, therefore, it is better to think about him who is the Wisdom of God.

THE PERSONALITY OF THE LEADER

On the human side, leadership is largely a matter of personality. This word seems to mean the sum and substance of all that is in the man. In other words, the secret of personality, or charm, is as elusive as quicksilver. One man from whom we expect little proves to be what his people call a born leader in worship. Another man from whom we expect everything good seems to lose his charm when he tries to lead. Not every lover of God and men is able to lead effectively in public worship. By watching the men who lead well, one discovers that each of them does so in a different way, but that they are practically all alike in at least five respects.

First, the true leader is careful about externals. He strives to dress and act like a gentleman. If he does so all the time, he finds it natural to be dignified and urbane in the hour of worship. Otherwise, he might seem stiff and insincere. Since he wishes to be presentable, and yet not conspicuous, he may prefer to wear the Geneva gown; but of course he complies with the best local custom. So does he make the most out of his voice, knowing that the voice is an index of a man's culture. Like Jowett or Spurgeon, every leader in worship should have a pleasing voice, clear and resonant, never loud and strident. Fortunately, a man's voice improves under the right sort of treatment. In these matters the minister ought to have a friendly adviser. This is one of many reasons why a man is often more effective as a leader in worship after he is happily married.

Second, and more important, the leader should have strong intellectual powers, highly developed in the schools. The test of a minister's intellect is largely in his ability to size up a situation, devise practical ways of doing what needs to be done, and then lead others in doing what he has planned. Any minister who has served for a while as a busy pastor, and then has gone into teaching, can testify that it often requires more intellectual ability to carry out one's program for the year's worship than it does to meet the problems of the classroom. Unfortunately, the schools cannot impart such intellectual ability, or even show a man how to use it in leading public worship. We are trying, however, to send out men who have brains enough to meet every situation as it arises.

Third, and most vital of all, thus far, is breadth and depth of emotional powers. Especially in the parts which we call priestly, public worship is largely the expression of feeling. How can the minister lead if he does not feel? This is true above all in prayer, and in administering the Sacrament; but it is true also in his relation to the music, and in his reading of the Scriptures. Hence the call is for sympathy, which is another name for Christian love in action. If a leader has what one may call sympathy with God, and likewise with the people, one by one, thus being able to put himself into the place of the man in the pew and look at the world through his eyes, this leader is almost certain to be effective. In other words, the man who is effective as a pastor is likely to be effective as a leader in worship, and for the same reason, because his heart is great and is overflowing with love.

Fourth, the leader should be a man of strong will power. The will is only another name for the entire personality in action. Many a man who is pleasing in his personality, with strong intellectual powers and breadth of sympathies, is not effective as a leader, because he lacks that dynamic quality sometimes known as "the drive." But that is not the word to use about leading in worship, for the man of God is dealing with sheep and lambs, not with horses and mules. He knows better than to drive sheep. As a leader, he has a strong sense of purpose and direction, with the ability to keep moving steadily through a service. Though he never becomes nervous or excited, he is able to communicate his own enthusiasm. He has the ability to attract and hold attention, whether by speech, by silence, or by symbol; the ability to express strong, deep emotions without losing his self-control, for if he did that once the people might fear that he would do it again; the ability to awaken the conscience and move the will of the worshiper Godwards. Who can begin to appraise the importance of the will in the leader of worship?

It requires power of will to meet many a situation properly. For instance, when a baby screams, one does nothing. When an aged person faints, one does something, but what? That depends on the circumstances. Ordinarily, one remains in the pulpit and leads the congregation, perhaps in silence, or else in song, while the officers care for the one who has fainted. When there is a cry of "Fire!" in a building which seems sure to burn, presence of mind and resourcefulness may avert tragic loss of life. At the auditorium in Winona Lake, in the summer of 1928, such leadership prevented a panic. Some person screamed, "Put it out!" Instead of a conflagration, there was only an old black cat; but everyone who is familiar with crowd psychology knows that reason has little to do with causing a panic. Religion, however, has much to do with averting such threatened disaster. By faith, the leader in worship can conquer his human fears, and lead others into safety. No man has any more powers of leadership than he can command in an emergency. Thank God, then, if you have a strong will! [7]

Fifth, and most difficult to discuss, is the imagination. This is the distinguishing characteristic of the artist as contrasted with the artisan. In adorning the ceiling of the Sistine Chapel in the Vatican, Michelangelo needed no more varied powers than the leader of public worship should employ as he strives to express the feelings of countless human beings. On the other hand, almost any artisan with the proper equipment could paint his part of the ceiling, and so can many a minister go through

[7] Cf. *The Life of John Wesley*, by C. T. Winchester, Macmillan, 1922, pp. 287-289.

THE FINE ART AND THE ARTIST

the forms of public worship without seeming to use his imagination. This is perhaps the one quality which is most likely to be lacking in the leader. Fortunately, however, the imagination is like almost every other gift of God; it develops through proper use. So if any man who is called to lead in worship will enter into each service imaginatively, by faith he will in time become a master of his fine art. Is not the Gospel itself a gift to the imagination?

Here, then, are five marks of the ideal leader. Each of the five is positive. Negatively, there is in his ways of leadership nothing to call attention to himself, either by elegance or slovenliness, by adornment or sheer ugliness. Here is nothing of conventional ministerial modesty, which says, "Please let us sing," or else, "Will you pray?" What if some wag replied, "No, I thank you, Sir, I wish to go home"? Here is no drillmaster, training his squad to run through semi-military maneuvers with mechanical skill. No, here is an artist, engaged in the calling which he loves more than life. He may not be great in the eyes of the world, which has never heard about most of its artists; but every minister who does his best in the leadership of worship is good in the eyes of God.

In the light of such lofty ideals, there is no room for self-display. In Dublin, on April 13, 1742, after the first public rendition of *The Messiah,* someone asked Handel how he had felt while composing the "Hallelujah Chorus." The artist replied, "I did think I did see all heaven open before me, and the great God himself." When Lord

29

Kinnoul complimented him on the entertainment which he had given the town, the composer said, "I should be sorry if I only entertained. I wish to make them better." What a motto for any man who aspires to become a master of the fine art of leading in worship! God first! The people second! Self third!

By this time, perhaps, someone is tempted to lose heart and wonder why he ever started out to do what is evidently impossible. If so, let him remember what Paul says about the heavenly treasure in earthen vessels.[8] At Cairo in the Museum of Egyptian Antiquities the curator once pointed out an earthen vessel which seemed devoid of beauty and worth. But when he turned on the light within, it proved to be a vase of alabaster, and it shone with a beauty as from God. So when the light of God's indwelling presence shines out through the leader in worship, he becomes a radiant Christian personality. Under God, that is the sort of leader whom many a parish is needing today.

[8] II Cor. 4:7.

the land to the descendants of the original owners. Thus the entire Hebrew system of worship was primarily for farmers.

Turning now to the second grand division of the Old Testament, we shall look directly only at the Psalms. With them we should consider the narrative portions of First and Second Chronicles. While these two books, which are really only one, receive scant attention from the student of history, partly because the emphasis is largely liturgical and homiletic, this very fact makes them useful to us here. Surely they came out of the Hebrew Church, and thus they show some of her ideals about public worship. The reason for thinking of Chronicles in connection with the Book of Psalms is because all these records show that there was in Old Testament times a large and growing emphasis upon sacred music.[3]

The Hebrew ideal concerning music in public worship was much like that which is increasingly popular among Protestant churches today. The Hebrews had their professional musicians, "the sons of Korah," with one chief musician, whom we may call "the minister of music." Even during the hard times under Ezra and Nehemiah there was regular provision for the maintenance of these musicians.[4] While there was more or less use of instruments, the chief reliance was upon choral singing. Often there was a choir, and sometimes it was larger than in any

[3] I Chron. 15:16-28; 16:4-42; II Chron. 5:12, 13, *et al.* Cf. *A Liturgical Study of the Psalter,* by C. C. Keet and G. H. Box, Macmillan, 1928, pp. 63-66, *et al.*
[4] Neh. 11:23; 12:47.

modern place of worship. At times the chorus included women as well as men. Much of the singing was in unison, as it often should be now. Less frequently, it was antiphonal, as one can see in the twenty-fourth psalm.

Yes, those Hebrews were a singing people, and their songs seem to have been almost wholly religious. When they were making a holy pilgrimage to Jerusalem, to celebrate one of the annual festivals, there was a daily procession with many sacred songs, such as the one hundred twenty-first psalm. In the course of years, those people assembled the five parts of their hymnal, the Book of Psalms. This is the supreme book of praise in the history of corporate religion, the only book of sacred song which the students of English at Princeton and Oxford rank among the masterpieces of world literature. Here is the most important book in the Old Testament, at least for the student of public worship.[5]

The third grand division, according to the arrangement in our English Bible, consists of the writings of the prophets. Here we seem at first to find little about public worship. Before me lies a popular book about the prophets, with an index covering five full pages; but there is no reference to public worship, music, prayer, or anything of the sort. But when we look at the writings themselves somewhat closely, we find a good deal about public worship. Indeed, the ideals of the prophets about the proper way to worship God in public seem much like our own, especially in the non-liturgical churches. Isaiah,

[5] Cf. *The Psalms as Liturgies*, by John P. Peters, Macmillan, 1922.

36

for example, believed in public worship with all his heart. Had not his own transforming experience come to him in terms of corporate worship? Doubtless that was one reason why he spent much of his time and energy in the vain attempt to reform the ways of public worship in Jerusalem and throughout Judah.

The same is largely true of other prophets. Isaiah's contemporary, Amos, for instance, is known to us chiefly because of what he said and did when the people of the Northern Kingdom were assembled for public worship at Bethel. Unfortunately, it was of the wrong kind. So did Jeremiah and the other prophets strive in vain to prevent the disintegration of the grand old Hebrew ideals concerning public worship. The Book of Malachi, for example, teaches that a revival of spiritual religion depends in large measure upon a reform in ways of corporate worship.

The one prophetic writer who has most to say about the subject is Ezekiel. While he is not especially popular with students of literary style, or with those who stress preaching rather than worship, his writings deserve careful attention. What concerns us now is the latter part of the book. In the first twenty-four chapters his spirit is severe, but in the second twenty-four there is more of kindliness and hope. The last nine chapters present visions of an ideal social order, in which everything is to center around the Temple. These chapters are difficult for us to understand, partly because the theory of worship is that which appears in Leviticus, with its ritual laws, and likewise

37

because the language of Ezekiel is that of mysterious symbolism. Perhaps the easiest way to come close to the spirit of Ezekiel's writings would be to cultivate the friendship of a devout rabbi in the orthodox Jewish Church, and then listen to what he says about the Holy Land as it ought to be according to the visions of Ezekiel. Unfortunately, some of the leaders of Zionism seem to be more intent upon selling salt and potash from the Dead Sea than upon praying for the fulfillment of Ezekiel's vision about the cleansing of those stagnant waters.[6] Under God, according to that vision, the hope for our old sin-cursed world is in the Church.

Thus we have looked at selected books in the three parts of the Old Testament. If we put all of these impressions together, we find that the Hebrews had lofty ideals about public worship. Although they did not live up to their ideals any better than we have lived up to ours, those ideals are of much concern to us, because in large measure they carry over into the New Testament, and thence into the Christian Church. According to those ideals, the two dominant notes in public worship are the forgiveness of sins and joy in the Lord. The two ought ever to come in this order. As soon as men got right with God, they were to enjoy each other. Thus their social life was to center round the Church.

Public worship in Old Testament days was an art. That worship was chiefly liturgical. Although those people were so childlike that they did not excel in other

---

[6] Ezek. 47:1-12.

38

arts, except in poetry, and that religious, they did surpass all other ancient peoples in the finest of all fine arts, that of public worship. Then, as now, there was danger that the art would overshadow the religion; but fortunately we can think of public worship as it shines out in the Psalms, and in some of the Prophets. By God's grace we can strive to carry these same ideals into the public worship of the Church today.

5 ways for experiencing

PUBLIC WORSHIP IN THE NEW TESTAMENT *different from O. T.*

The teachings of the New Testament are even more largely indirect. One reason is because the New Testament writers were nearly all Hebrews, and thus they took for granted that the permanent values of Old Testament worship would abide in the Christian Church. While the New Testament clearly does away with the sacrifices of the Old Testament, and with the mediating priesthood, as well as the one central sanctuary, these changes had to do largely with form. In spirit, the worship of the New Testament was much like that of the Old Testament, but higher.

So let us think about the ways of public worship in each of the three grand divisions in this smaller and more precious hemisphere of that world which we call the Bible. We may think of the first five books as constituting the first unit, for here are the facts on which we base our faith in Christ. In the Epistles, we find the inspired interpretation of these facts. In the Revelation is the vision of that ideal social order when the kingdoms of this world shall become the Kingdom of our Christ.

In the Gospels and the Book of Acts, there is a good deal about the Temple. According to the Gospels, the Lord Jesus loved and revered the Temple. There as a babe he had been publicly presented before the Lord; there at the age of twelve he had been found among the doctors of the Law; there as a man he evidently joined with his countrymen in celebrating the festivals of the Hebrew Year. So much did he love the Temple that he seems to have cleansed it twice; surely he cleansed it once.[7] "Is it not written, My house shall be called of all nations the house of prayer?" In like manner did the Apostles, including Paul, set the example of due regard for the Temple. Doubtless they did so partly because it stood in the eyes of the people as the symbol of public worship.

Much more important than the Temple was the synagogue. Without a certain appreciation of the broad facts about the synagogue, one could scarcely hope to understand the prominence of public worship in the days of our Lord and his Apostles. The synagogue seems to have sprung up during the Exile. By the time our Lord was ready to begin his public ministry, the synagogue was almost everywhere in the world around the Mediterranean, especially in the Holy Land. Every such meeting place stood for public worship, and for teaching, as well as for old-fashioned friendliness. Here, then, was the

[7] Mark 11:15-18; cf. John 2:13-17.

40

normal place to begin the evangelization of any community. In Nazareth today there is a synagogue which is doubtless much like the one where our Lord preached his sermon from the words of Isaiah about the Gospel to the poor.[8] Since he made Capernaum the center of his ministry in Galilee, he must often have been with God's people in such a synagogue as the one which the archaeologists have unearthed at Tell Hum, the probable site of Capernaum.

These facts are of concern to us because the early Christian Church took over the synagogue forms of worship in large measure.[9] In the synagogue the regular Sabbath service called for the Shema, which was a sort of Hebrew Creed;[10] more or less music; eighteen or nineteen prayers, often reduced to six; the reading of the lesson from the Law, and of another from the Prophets; and the exposition of the Scriptures. There was a regular leader; but there was no need of a priest, because there was no sacrifice. The exposition was largely didactic, not rhetorical. The speaker stood up to read, but he sat down to preach—standing when the word was from God and sitting when it was from himself.

In various forms the worship of the Jewish synagogue persists today, and so one can study the background of our Christian worship. Under the leadership of Rabbi Wise

[8] Isa. 61:1, 2a; Luke 4:14-30. Cf. *The Life and Times of Jesus the Messiah,* by Alfred Eldersheim, Longmans, Green, 1886, II, 430-450.

[9] Cf. *The Jewish Background of the Christian Liturgy,* by W. O. E. Oesterley, Oxford Press, 1925.

[10] Deut. 6:4-9, *et al.*

in New York, or Rabbi Fineshriber in Philadelphia, Jewish worship shows the possibilities latent in the public reading of the Scriptures. There is a minister of music, known as the cantor, and the singing from the choir loft is sometimes like that of angels in glory. The period of worship is marked by a sense of rhythm and balance, as well as movement, which ought ideally to lead up to a sermon about the Messiah. Instead of that, one is likely to hear an eloquent address lauding the New Deal. Sometimes there seems to be a gulf of at least nineteen hundred years between the old worship and "the new preaching." Most of us Gentiles could learn more from the worship than from the sermon.

Let us turn now to the Gospels. It would be profitable to read them, one by one, to note how large a place public worship occupied in the experience of our Lord and his disciples. This is especially true of the Fourth Gospel. It alone tells about our Lord's conversation with the woman at the well,[11] where he explained to her the heart of all that we Christians believe about public worship. In this same Gospel is our only record of what our Lord said in the Temple about himself as the Water of Life.[12] The most precious chapters in this Gospel are those which tell about the Upper Room.[13] In that Upper Room our Lord taught his disciples to remember him by taking the Sacrament. Though the group was small, the principles of Christian worship

[11] John 4: 19-24.   [12] John 7:37-39.
[13] John 13-17.

shine out clearly. While many of us hold to conservative ideas about these records in the Gospels, all that concerns us now is that they surely came out from the heart of the early Christian Church.

In a high sense the Christian Church was born at Pentecost. That experience probably came in the Upper Room, where a hundred twenty believers were assembled for worship. If the experience was in the Temple, as some believe, still the Holy Spirit descended while the disciples worshiped together.[14] Out from that experience of worship came the most amazing evangelistic and missionary movement in the history of the Christian Church. To trace the course of that movement until at last the Apostle Paul found himself at Rome is one of the purposes in the Book of Acts.

Here again is an attractive opportunity for Bible reading, to learn how largely public worship bulked in the experience of those early Christians. For example, at Philippi in a meeting for social worship the Christian Church began her work of transforming Europe.[15] Under God, that work was possible in many places because the synagogue had partly prepared the way. Perhaps one reason why Paul succeeded in Corinth much better than in Athens was because there had been at least one synagogue in Corinth, whereas there seems to have been none in Athens. In short, both evangelism and missions owe their rise largely to public worship.

A reading of the Epistles will confirm this impression

[14] Acts 2:1-4.   [15] Acts 16:9-15.

concerning the importance of public worship among the early Christians. In fact, the Epistles themselves had an important part in those gatherings of believers. For example, the twelfth chapter of Romans shows that the believers were to assemble for worship, and that there they would hear the reading of this message. First Corinthians is largely concerned with practical guidance about the proper behavior in public worship. Ephesians appears to have been a circular letter, which went from one congregation to another, and so contained no personal greetings. Thus one might run through the Epistles and come to the conclusion that in the corporate life of the early Christian Church everything centered around public worship. Like the Church herself, almost every Epistle was born and nurtured in worship.

The same is true, perhaps to a still greater degree, in the Apocalypse, which in its way is the most Christian book in the Bible—that is, the one where the Living Christ is most nearly all in all. Partly for this reason the book is one long succession of mysteries, for in its upper reaches our faith is not so simple as we sometimes suppose. But it is clear that in the second and the third chapter our Lord is speaking to the churches, evidently as they assemble for public worship. In the American Revised Version, scattered here and there throughout the book, are twelve passages which the editors have caused to stand out separately by indentation. These passages are the most lyrical in the book, and probably they show the sort of songs in use by the Christian Church towards the end of the first century. In short, the Book of Revelation yields inspiration and power when we think of it as reflecting the spirit in which the early Church engaged in the worship of the Living Lord.

A reading of the New Testament as a whole leaves the impression that never before or since has the spirit of worship manifested itself so gloriously as among those early Christians.[16] Of course they were not perfect, but in at least five respects their ways of public worship were more nearly ideal than those in the Hebrew Church. In other words, while the Hebrews were to a large measure a childlike people, the early Christians had the sort of worship which one would expect to find among mature men and women who love Jesus Christ. Here are five facts about their worship.

First, there was a lack of emphasis upon externals. Instead of the Old Testament emphasis upon a certain place and certain times, certain rites and certain duties, there was a feeling that worship is a matter of the heart, that wherever the people of God gather together there they can worship him. Even at the mother church in Jerusalem the equipment seems to have been meager, partly because the members were not wealthy. As a rule, the bands of believers here and there around the Mediterranean worshiped in private homes. Thus their worship would be much like that of a mission station in Iran or

[16] See *The Spirit of Worship,* by Friedrich Heiler, Hodder & Stoughton, London, 1928, p. 21.

Chosen, where the local Church of Christ may seem like a little oasis in the surrounding desert of heathenism.

Second, there was a new sense of freedom to worship God without the use of fixed forms. In the Apostolic Church the regular meeting for edification was much like that of the synagogue, with prayers and benedictions, singing of psalms, readings from the Law and the Prophets, and doubtless also from the Apostles, and exposition of the Scriptures. This is what we may call the Word-of-God Service. On the first day of the week there was also another sort of worship, which we may call the Thanksgiving Service. Here the Lord's Supper was the culmination. It took the place of the Hebrew Passover as the supreme expression of gratitude to God for redemption. But where the Hebrews partook of the Passover only once a year, the early Christians seem to have celebrated the Sacrament every Lord's Day. In various parts of the Mediterranean world the forms of worship seem to have varied. Surely there is in the New Testament nothing which prescribes or suggests the use of fixed forms, but neither is there anything which forbids or discourages such use. The rule of the Holy Spirit seems to be, "Love God, and then worship according to your heart's desire." In such worship there is perfect freedom.

Third, in the worship of the New Testament Church, as contrasted with the rites of the Hebrews, there was much more emphasis on the people, and much less upon the leader. When the people of God became conscious that the coming of the Lord Jesus had set them free

46

from the obligation to offer animal sacrifices, and that his death guaranteed to every believer the right to become a priest of the Living God, worship began to be democratic. This tendency had been at work among the prophets and in the synagogue; but only after the death and the resurrection of our Lord did the people of God become conscious of their holy privileges as priests. On the human side, this change of emphasis is perhaps the most noteworthy of the five characteristics now before us. Of course the New Testament ways of worship made a place for leadership, somewhat like that to which we are accustomed; but even when the leader of worship was Peter, John, or Paul, he and the people knew that all of them together were priests of the Living God. What a revolutionary truth! Surely it deserves more attention than it receives, both in our sermons and in our prayers of thanksgiving.

Fourth, there was a corresponding change of spirit, so that one thinks of worship in the Apostolic Church as radiant. This radiance seems to have begun on the first Easter Day, and to have come to its most glorious corporate expression on Pentecost. As a consequence, the Jews who were assembled in the Holy City for the most popular festival of their Church Year thought that the Christians were intoxicated.[17] In a sense the critics were correct; those early Christians were God-intoxicated. This seems to be what Paul means when he warns believers in Ephesus and elsewhere not to be drunk with

[17] Acts 2:13-18. Cf. Eph. 5:18-21.

47

wine, but to be filled with the Spirit, so as to sing acceptably in the worship of God. Hence we should think of Pentecost, and more normal times of worship, as noteworthy for their enthusiasm. This word enthusiasm literally means "God in us." When God is in his people, as he wishes to be, they are inspired, and their worship is full of apostolic fervor.

Such a congregation is in a state of continuous revival. In days of revival there is a new and increasing delight in prayer, a new and fervent expression of joy in song, and a new emphasis upon the preaching of the Word. Ordinarily we think of the Apostolic Churches in terms of Christian doctrine, or else Christian ethics; but their doctrines seem to have been largely the expression of their growing Christian experience in worship, and ideally their ways of living were in accordance with the light which they saw in the House of the Lord. When devout believers are in vital touch with the Living Christ, and constantly rejoicing in the privilege of worship, they are glad to believe all that he makes known to them about himself as the center of Christian belief and service.

Fifth and last among these marks of the Apostolic Church was the new access of power. Of course this was the power of the Holy Spirit, but what concerns us is that he came in power at Pentecost; that is, in public worship. As a result, those men who had often seemed weak as water became mighty in word and in deed. Here is the secret of power in preaching, power in soul winning, power in the extension of the Kingdom throughout the world. This is largely what we mean when we speak about the lost radiance of the Apostolic Church. If so, we can find that radiance where we seem to have lost it; that is, in public worship of the Living Christ. (Public worship is no acceptable substitute for private devotions, or anything else in the Christian life; but neither is anything else an acceptable substitute for public worship. Wherever that is as it should be, the other means of grace likewise flourish. They all belong together. All of them together, under God, explain the radiance and the power of the Apostolic Church.[18])

Looking back now, we note that public worship filled a large place at the very center of religion in Old Testament times, and a still larger place in the early days of Christianity as reflected in the New Testament. To the truth, the inspiration, and the vision derived from public worship, the Apostolic Church seems largely to have owed her power for heroic living and heroic service, even unto death. In public worship was the fountainhead of those living waters which we know as evangelism and missions. Here too was the chief reason, on the human side, for the writing and the preservation of the books in the New Testament. Practically every one of them came into being in connection with public worship, because the people of God needed such inspired guidance in knowing what to believe concerning God the Father, the Son, and

[18] See *Christian Worship in the Primitive Church*, by Alex B. McDonald, T. & T. Clark, Edinburgh, 1934.

the Holy Spirit, and likewise what duty God requires of man, both as a child of the Heavenly Father, and as a servant of his fellow men.

This is the sort of public worship which the fathers sought to restore at the Reformation, and which we should revive in a present-day renaissance. The only sort of public worship which will enable us to meet the needs of our day, and under God, to solve its problems, is that which centers in Christ as the Son of God. Instead of crying out, therefore, "Back to the ways in which our fathers worshiped God!" let us rather take as our motto, "Onward to the Living Christ!" But we shall find him where the reformers found him, in the open pages of the Bible.

CHAPTER III

THE STRUGGLE OF RELIGION WITH ART

IN the history of the Church there has been a constant struggle between religion and art, to determine which shall prevail in public worship. As in the study of any other art, the best approach to worship is through history. (That is one reason why we began with the Bible.) There is the fountainhead of Christian worship. After leaving the Bible, the stream followed a course which no one could have predicted. Today it is still a question what forms the worship of the future will assume. Whatever the forms, they should be in keeping with the evangelical tradition, according to which our worship is more or less in line with that of the Apostolic Church. Thus the oldest in Christian worship is the best, if by the oldest we understand that which is closest to the Living Christ.

In such a historical study, the temptation is to wander off into certain bypaths. For instance, it would be well worth while to ascertain how many of the notable controversies in the history of the Church have arisen in connection with public worship. It would be still more to the point to learn how many of the religious persecutions have been directly concerned with freedom in worship. While the recent persecutions in Mexico, Germany,

51

Chosen, and elsewhere, have assumed forms different from those in other times, the basic causes of persecution, now as then, are usually bound up with matters of public worship. For another example, think of the situation in Spain. So it seems that the devil is able to use even the worship of Christ as the means of fomenting passion and strife.

While the trail on which we are setting forth is not so exciting, the result should be a clearer understanding of what it means to worship God in public. So let us think about the history of the struggle between religion and art, the outcome of the struggle in so far as it has led to definite decisions, and the practical value of these facts today.

THE HISTORY OF THE STRUGGLE

It is possible here only to introduce the subject, with the hope of leading to further study.[1] Every student of church history knows that in public worship of the first century the artistic element was subordinate to the spiritual, and that before the beginning of the Middle Ages, about 476 A.D., the artistic element seems to have triumphed. The change from the orderly freedom of the Apostolic Church to the artistic forms of what we know as the Roman Catholic Church seems to have begun in the second century, increased during the third, largely prevailed in the fourth, and still more so in the fifth. From

[1] See *A History of Christian Worship,* by Oscar Hardman, Cokesbury, 1937.

52

that time until the Reformation, there was no difficulty in seeing that public worship was an art, but sometimes men were tempted to forget that it was religious.

In these matters of worship, the Roman Catholic Church owes a vast deal to Cyprian, Bishop of Carthage about the middle of the third century.[2] After his day there was increased emphasis upon the Visible Church as the seat of authority, the church building as the place for public worship, the importance of set times and set forms, as well as the observance of the Church Year. Above all, there was the development of the Mass, which is probably the supreme triumph of art in worship. When stripped of its artistic refinements, the Mass is simply a certain way of celebrating the Holy Communion. But what a way! In Oberammergau many visitors are even more impressed by the spectacle of the Mass in the village church at five o'clock in the morning than by the Passion Play which proceeds through the long hours of morning and afternoon. The Mass is religious drama in its most highly developed artistic forms.

This movement towards artistic forms meant going back from New Testament liberty to Old Testament rites, which had been prescribed for a childlike people. The authority for these changes from New Testament simplicity came from the Church, which is to the devout Catholic a sort of Supreme Court in all matters of religion and life. Instead of the simplicity which we Protestants

[2] Cf. *Epistle to the Philippians,* by J. B. Lightfoot, Macmillan, 1891, pp. 240-250.

associate with Christ, there was a growing tendency to exalt the externals in public worship. Hence the artistic forms appealed more and more to the five senses of child-like people. There were vestments and bells, ablutions and symbolic actions, frequent changes in posture, as well as processions with the cross, prayers for the dead, and other well-known ways of appealing to pious hearts. In fact, some scholar should prepare a thesis showing how the Roman Catholic ways of worship in the Middle Ages grew largely out of Old Testament rites, but with count-less refinements, all in the interests of sacred art.

These artistic ways of worship, centering in sacrifice, called for a mediating priesthood. That in turn led to the formation of a hierarchy of priests, who wished to hold in their hands the powers of state as well as church, and even to determine the eternal destinies of sinful mor-tals. What Aaron and his sons and the Levites had been in the Hebrew Church, all of that, and vastly more, the bishops, the priests, and the deacons strove to become in the Catholic Church. As for the pope, at least in the eyes of the unlearned, his powers must have seemed like those of our Lord. This was a departure from the ideas of the Old Testament. So is the custom of having the Mass in Latin. One would expect it to be in Greek or Hebrew, if not in the vernacular of the people who wor-ship. Doubtless one reason why it is in Latin is because of the sonorous quality of that tongue, and because trans-lation almost always weakens the literary charm of any piece of literature. In other words, art seemed for a while to have won its way to the seat of authority in Christian worship.

The Protestant Reformation strove to restore the Biblical balance between religion and art. The purpose was to recover the spirit of New Testament worship, much as one might remove the handiwork of later artists who have tried to improve a masterpiece by Da Vinci or Michelangelo. Just as our Lord cleansed the Temple, so after fifteen hundred years of increasing incrustations, he raised up leaders to reform Christian worship. But sometimes they went too far. With all of its accretions the Roman Catholic Mass contained elements which some of us Protestants are only beginning to appreciate. While we thank God for the Reformation, and rejoice in the liberty of worship which it gave back to those who wished to be free, we regret that the more extreme reformers sometimes became iconoclasts, and that their liberty led to license. It was not so, however, with Martin Luther, for he had been cradled in the arms of the Roman Catholic Church.

THE OUTCOME OF THE STRUGGLE

In a sense, the struggle is still going on, and perhaps it will for years. It has been wholly within the Christian Church. Now that there is a far more deadly struggle between the church and the state in many a land, such as Russia, all of us Christians see that we are on the same side, if in different regiments. So let us close our eyes to the differences between our Protestant ways and those of the Catholics, whether Roman or Greek. Merely for the sake of seeing where we stand, let us note three trends in contemporary Protestant worship. Of course there are all sorts of intermediate positions. But purely for convenience, we shall think of the right wing, the left wing, and the central position.

On the right wing are those who follow Martin Luther's ideas about public worship. His ideas at the Reformation were much like those of Peter at Pentecost. Each of those reforms called for the use of the vernacular, exaltation of Christ, and emphasis upon preaching, especially the preaching of two doctrines, justification by faith, not by works, and the priesthood of believers. As a reformer, not an iconoclast, each of those men strove to retain and use all that was worthy in the system of worship which he was striving to reform. Luther, for example, strove to retain the beauty and power of the Mass, but he insisted that it should be in the mother tongue of the people. So today the forms of worship in the Lutheran churches almost everywhere embody much of the artistic beauty of the Mass. The ways of worship among our Lutheran brethren deserve to be much better known.

Over in England the Reformation took a somewhat different course, which resulted in the well-known majestic forms in the *Book of Common Prayer*. While opinions may differ about which of these two ways is the better, the Lutheran or the Episcopalian, it is clear that the two belong together in our right wing. In recent years the trend in many other Protestant churches has been somewhat steadily towards a modified form of such a liturgical service. In the Methodist Episcopal Church, for example, there has been a movement towards such semi-liturgical worship. That is not strange, for as the name indicates, the Methodist Church came out of the Episcopal Church. The separation came in no small measure because of John Wesley's custom of preaching to the common people in the fields. Here again, public worship is close to the heart of evangelism, as well as to the causes of ecclesiastical separation.

On the left wing among us Protestants are the Friends, or Quakers, some of the Baptists, and other bodies which seem to care little for artistic forms in worship. The course of time has tended to bring each of these bodies over towards the center. In some of the meetinghouses of the Friends the worship is much like that among the Methodists. But here and there, the simple ways of the fathers still survive among the Friends, many of whom live in and near Philadelphia. These ways deserve to be much more widely known. Who, for instance, can ever forget the experience of seeing a marriage service in a Quaker meetinghouse? Many students of public worship feel that the ways among the Friends are apostolic, not only in their simplicity, but also in their effect upon the worshipers, with their love of peace and their zeal for helping the victims of war.

The central group includes perhaps the largest number of Protestants. Here are the large majority of the Baptists, the Congregationalists, who are now united with the

Christian Church, the Church of Christ, the Reformed Churches, and the Presbyterians. Here, of course, are the Methodists.[3] But why bunch all these diverse groups together? Why not include others? Because we wish merely to make the central position clear. It is that in Christian worship there should be a blending of religion and art; that is, of Christian liberty and artistic forms, with the emphasis ever upon the religion and the liberty.

This was essentially the theory of John Calvin. If in some respects Luther's ideas about public worship were like those of Peter, and if John Wesley's insistence upon Christian experience was much like that of the Apostle for whom he was named, there is a sense in which Calvin strove to put into effect the Pauline ideals about public worship. These analogies are open to all sorts of objections, but it is a fact that in the Protestant churches today the forms of worship owe more to the influence of Luther, Wesley, and Calvin than to any other three men since the days of Peter, John, and Paul.[4]

Calvin attached untold importance to public worship, but from a point of view unlike that of Luther. Where Luther wished to preserve the artistic forms of the Catholic Church in so far as they did not contravene the teachings of Scripture, Calvin favored the rejection of what the Scriptures did not clearly enjoin. Under his leadership public worship in Geneva became notable for

[3] Cf. *Vital Elements of Public Worship,* by J. Ernest Rattenbury, Epworth Press, London, 1936, pp. 75-98.
[4] Cf. *Revivals, Their Laws and Leaders,* James Burns, Hodder & Stoughton, London, 1919.

its emphasis upon the majesty of God, the sinfulness of man, and the wonders of redeeming grace. In other words, those ways of worship were largely objective, sometimes too largely so. There was much emphasis upon the singing of the Psalms. That part of the service is said to have been inspiring. There was mighty emphasis, also, upon the exposition of the Bible from the pulpit. There was increased freedom, as well as responsibility, for the minister. While Calvin himself attached relatively small importance to fixed rites, he believed in conforming with local custom. While he preferred forms which were simple, he believed in order, and he would have been astounded at such lack of dignity as obtains among some of his followers today.[5]

After the days of Calvin, many who tried to follow him in his theology practically forsook his ideas about worship; and thus they found themselves almost without artistic forms. In fact, they rebelled against the use of such forms in worship, not because they were fixed, but because they were forced. In other words, where public worship becomes a matter of bitter controversy, leading to persecution, and even to war, the reaction is unwholesome. But why rake over those dead coals? The facts are fairly well known to most Presbyterian ministers,[6] and may not be specially interesting to others. The gratifying fact is that the majority of Presbyterian ministers in the United States are anxious to share in a revival of public worship

[5] *John Calvin*, by Williston Walker, Putnam's, 1906, pp. 222-225.
[6] See *The Worship of the Scottish Reformed Church*, by William Mc-Millan, Jas. Clarke & Co., London, 1931.

as a fine art, according to the ideals of John Calvin and John Knox.

While the old warfare about ways of worship is largely a matter of history, many a minister who gladly takes his place in the central group feels that the question is not yet settled. There is much still to be said for the kind of public worship which exalts artistic forms, and likewise for that which stresses substance rather than artistic form; but when one tries to secure the advantages of two contrasting ways of worship, one is likely to suffer the common fate of the man who compromises. Thus one may lose the strength of the service which stresses substance, without securing the beauty of the one which exalts art. This is doubtless why Harris E. Kirk of Baltimore insists that we must choose between stressing the prophet and the Bible, or else the priest and the altar.[7] His own sympathies are strongly on the side of the prophet and the Bible.

Is it any wonder that many a minister is perplexed, and is halting in the presence of these three theories about worship, being definitely committed to no one of them? Sometimes he feels like singing one of the "hymns for those at sea." If he followed his heart, he might go to the right, with the liturgical group; if he consulted his reason, he might turn to the left, with the non-liturgical group; probably he will make up his mind to walk in the middle road. But if so, let him be able to do it with a clear conscience, for no one can lead effectively in public

[7] *The Spirit of Protestantism*, Cokesbury, 1930, pp. 199-233.

worship while wondering whether he should not be doing it all in a different way. So let us try to appraise each of the three broad theories about public worship as a fine art.

THREE WAYS OF LEADING IN WORSHIP

The simplest path of approach seems to be that of taking up the arguments for the use of a liturgy, the arguments against such use, and the arguments for the use of an optional liturgy. By the word liturgy one means the use in worship of fixed artistic forms prescribed by the authority of the Church; by non-liturgical worship, the comparative absence of such forms, whether prescribed or not; by an optional liturgy, the partial use of artistic forms by the minister, according to the ideals of his church, but without any feeling of compulsion.

The argument for the use of a liturgy is threefold, relating to the clergyman, the congregation, and the Kingdom. First, the use of a liturgy is said to be a boon to the clergyman of limited ability. There is a widespread feeling that if the man at the altar is a master of his fine art, his people benefit most when he is largely free from the use of fixed forms; but that if he is a man of limited ability, he renders the most acceptable service when he keeps to the trail marked out by men of greater ability. The assumption seems to be that our Protestant churches ought to use artistic forms because many of our leaders are men of mediocre powers.[8]

[8] Cf. *Concerning Prayer,* by B. H. Streeter *et al.,* Macmillan, 1916, pp. 285, 286.

If this were the only argument, the case would soon be settled. Public worship is for the glory of God, and the blessing of his people, not for the sake of affording the minister a livelihood. Surely the Church today does not need a host of ministers. Hence it seems to be the part of wisdom to train only the young man with marked ability. Some of our seminaries are admitting only about half of the college graduates who apply. Consequently, the standard of ministerial ability seems to be rising. While the strongest men are no abler than a generation ago, the average is much higher, and the best is yet to be. Under God, the continued existence of the Christian Church in many a land seems to depend on her having the right sort of ministerial leadership. If so, none but our best young manhood is good enough for leadership in public worship.

Second, and much more vital, is the advantage to the congregation. The use of artistic forms does much to attract boys and girls, as well as to hold them throughout their most impressionable years. The singing affords the boys an opportunity to take an active part in the leadership of worship, and the dramatic action appeals to the girls as much as to the boys. So do stately forms appeal to the imagination of childlike people, and countless young folk. At West Point the sons of many different churches use the *Book of Common Prayer,* and so become Episcopalians for life. In college and at the university young men and women become accustomed to worship in the beauty of holiness, and when they return to their homes the worship there may seem barren.

The use of artistic forms likewise appeals to older men and women of refined sensibilities. With increasing culture and love of the fine arts has come a growing dissatisfaction with ugliness in the worship of God. Such people tell us that the use of artistic forms sets them free from the minister's whims and moods, as well as his grammatical blunders and verbal infelicities. The most extreme instance may be that of a zealous young parson whose funeral oration led up to this climactic deliverance concerning the person whose body lay before him in the casket: "This is only the shell; the nut has gone." In another oratorical effort, he said about the departed damsel, "She was a peach."

In a community where this sort of thing is the only alternative, is it any wonder that the most refined people choose to worship in the little Gothic church which has a historic liturgy? Such friends feel that their artistic forms insure a service with dignity and reserve, order and balance, rhythm and progress, comprehensiveness and quiet charm. In such worship they have a sense of restfulness and peace, self-forgetfulness and outgoing love. They insist that some of us overintellectualize and over-energize our leadership in prayer and song, as well as our preaching and our sacraments, so that the morning hour often leaves the people weary in body, if not sick at heart. In the more artistic ways of worship, the people are not supposed to think long about any one person,

63

whether at the altar or in the pew, for they are all bound together in the bundle of life with the Lord Jesus and the saints of every age. In short, such worship is for the sake of the people, and they think that they ought to know best how they wish to worship.

The third argument, and the most vital of all, relates to the advancement of the Kingdom. This is the heart of the entire case for the use of artistic forms. At their best they tend to exalt the universal elements in Christianity. Those who follow a prayer by Chrysostom ought to be largely free from thoughts of the time and the place, as well as from worries about immediate problems and pressing needs. Where some of us seem to go to church to think about our troubles, these friends try to forget about them. They hope to be lifted up towards heaven, so that by faith they may bask in the sunlight of God's love for all mankind.

Such ways of worship tend to exalt the Church, not the minister. In Columbus, Ohio, three congregations used to be known as Dr. Palmer's Church, Dr. Britan's Church, and Dr. Hindman's Church. But no one ever thought of Trinity Episcopal Church as belonging to its rector, or of Grace Lutheran Church as less important than its pastor. These very names are suggestive of the fact that the church stands for the Trinity, and for Divine Grace. Whereas the "preacher" may invite people to come into the auditorium and listen to him, the clergyman asks his friends to come into the sanctuary and worship God. While the preacher may at times attract the larger

64

throng, the clergyman keeps on stressing public worship, especially the Sacrament, and rejoicing in holy symbols. Such worship seems to him to promote the interests of the Kingdom.

In such use of artistic forms there is a strong appeal to the religious emotions. While these ways of worship often appeal to the man who thinks, they do so largely because he also has a heart. Where one person can follow the Christmas star, which guides those who love to think, perhaps a score prefer to join in the Yuletide song with those who feel. Instead of using the hour leading up to the Eucharist as a time for a heavy doctrinal sermon, or even for launching the Annual Every-Member Canvass —as some of us have done—the liturgical churches believe that when they worship God they should not be striving for something immediately practical. They feel that the advancement of the Kingdom depends largely upon keeping public worship spiritual.

The use of artistic forms tends to exalt God, not the man in the pew. In adoration and confession, thanksgiving and petition, supplication and dedication, he should keep looking up to God. In the course of years, like Michelangelo, he should have the upward look. During the public reading of the Scriptures—not in listening to arguments about them, as though they needed human defence—he should learn to look up. Above all, in the proper observance of the Church Year he should learn to think of time and eternity in relation to Jesus Christ. During the months leading up to Christmas, and then on past Easter to Pentecost, the worshiper should come face to face with Christ as Saviour and Lord.

In the presence of such a threefold argument, and of other reasons which are worthy of note,[9] why do many of us not confine our worship to forms prescribed by our various churches? Our answer, likewise, is threefold. We begin with the Bible, whereas the liturgical friends begin with the Church. First of all, we find in the Scriptures no basis for the use of prescribed prayers, however artistic. We feel the need of fixed forms when we sing together, and in other parts of public worship, notably in administering the Sacrament, but not when we pray together for blessings which concern us here and now. So we are glad to find that in the Bible no prayer is prescribed, except a benediction. While we often repeat the Lord's Prayer, we know that such a use is purely optional. Strongly do we feel that even the most artistic rites, imposed upon a congregation from without, even though the power were vested in worthy hands, would be foreign to the spirit and the ideals of the New Testament. "Where the Spirit of the Lord is, there is liberty."[10]

On the other hand, as we often forget, there is in the New Testament nothing to forbid or even discourage the use of artistic forms in Christian worship. While those words of Paul about liberty seem to refer to public worship, they surely would not have deterred the Christians

---

[9] See *Ecclesiastical Polity*, by Richard Hooker, ed. by R. Bayne, Macmillan, 1902, V, 121-184; and *Apology for Authorized and Set Forms of Liturgy*, by Bp. Jeremy Taylor, ed. by R. Heber, London, 1828, VII, 319-390.

[10] II Cor. 3:17*b*.

in Corinth from using in the Word-of-God Service a prayer to which they had grown accustomed in the synagogue. And so today, since many of our friends find peace and joy in the use of artistic forms which their churches prescribe, we should thank God. So should we assure the younger men in our own churches that they are free to use artistic forms without being untrue to the fathers of the Reformation, as they in turn were not disloyal to the liberty guaranteed by the Scriptures.

Our second answer is that we find in the history of the Christian Church no reason for confining our worship to the use of liturgical forms. If we read the facts rightly, in the Apostolic and the post-Apostolic ages the Church was much more spiritual and powerful than in the fifth century; in the Middle Ages the Church suffered so much from highly standardized ways of worship that there had to be a Reformation, which had as much to do with worship as with doctrine and morals; and in the modern world the churches of Continental Europe and Latin America, notably in Russia, Spain and Mexico, have suffered so much from excessive use of liturgical forms that there has been popular revolt, even revolution. "By their fruits ye shall know them."

Of course the facts are not so simple as we make them seem. Many elements have entered in to complicate each national situation. In Russia under the Czar, as in Spain under Alphonso, or in Mexico under Diaz, the ways of liturgical worship were not so worthy as in the Lutheran Churches of Northern Europe, or in the Estab-

67

blished Church of England. Still it would be difficult to point to non-liturgical churches which have caused entire nations to try to live without religion, as France tried to do for a while after her Revolution. But why look across the sea? Look at Mexico, and some of the other nations to the south. When President John A. Mackay was laboring among university students in Mexico and South America, he could almost never begin by asking them to worship God, doubtless because forms had become obnoxious. In days to come this leader hopes that those noble young gentlemen will enjoy the public worship of God; but when that time comes, the worship will not be highly liturgical.

It is surely fair to think of the liturgical movement in its most highly developed form, and likewise to study its by-products. One of them is the growth of a priestly hierarchy, thus widening the gulf between the altar and the pew, a gulf which did not exist in the Apostolic Church. Another by-product is the comparative neglect of preaching. According to the Apostle, it pleased God to save sinners through what men termed the foolishness of preaching.[11] In many parts of the world, where there is no preaching, the people perish. A third by-product is the substitution of art for religion. It is no accident that the occasion of the Reformation was the selling of indulgences to aid in building Saint Peter's at Rome. From that time to this, while the sons of the reformers have been trying to keep art in their religious forms, the sons

[11] I Cor. 1:18-21.

68

of the Roman Church have been striving to keep religion in their artistic forms.

On a typical Sunday morning in Saint Peter's, while a few of the faithful are striving to worship God, hosts of tourists are milling about among the masterpieces of sacred art. It is easy to blame us Americans for such conditions; but the fact remains that we should let such conditions influence us when we read what the books say about the superiority of liturgical forms, especially in the Roman Catholic Church. According to our interpretation of Christian liberty, they are free to follow the ways which their fathers prescribed; but we do not see any reason for so confining our public worship.

Our third answer is the most practical, and the most positive. We hold to our ways of worship because we love them. Theoretically, we understand the arguments for the use of liturgical forms. Frankly, we wonder if we are able to answer those arguments; at least the books most worth reading are on the side of liturgical worship. When we visit liturgical churches which are true to their ideals, we enter with joy into their beautiful and majestic ways of worship. But all the while we know that neither their ways nor our ways have any monopoly of the advantages. Common sense should teach us that men and women of different backgrounds and different temperaments should not be forced to worship together in any one way. In many a village, for instance, the practical reason why there are three or four struggling little meetinghouses where there might theoretically be only one inclusive church, is because people differ in their ideas of worship. Hence the obstacles to church union are likely to be liturgical, rather than doctrinal or administrative.

Why should we not love our own ways of worship? While they are by no means perfect, they often bring us close to God. We are glad that present-day Christians have almost ceased quarreling among themselves, even about the things which matter most. Likewise are we glad that our Heavenly Father is always ready to hear us when we pray with the simplicity which was dear to our fathers and mothers. If anyone protests that this third answer is no argument, but only the expression of a sentiment which does more credit to our feelings than to our intelligence, perhaps that is ture. But since worship is primarily a matter of Christian feeling, it would be strange if we did not listen to the voice of our Christian experience.

Thus we have passed in review three lines of argument for the use of liturgical forms in public worship, and three lines of argument against the use of such prescribed forms. In any case, the objection is not against forms as artistic, but as fixed. A disinterested reader might conclude that the historic struggle has now led to a stalemate, so that the opposing sides agree to differ, and still be friends. That is largely true. Meanwhile, in all the churches, at home and abroad, we Christians are facing critical days, and we are not ready. We all need God, and so we need more vital ways of worship. We have considered both the liturgical answer to our question, and the non-liturgical,

70

only to find each of them wanting. As a rule, each is weak where the other is strong. So we now turn to the optional liturgy, which strives to secure the advantages of the other two ways and avoid their disadvantages.

The case for the optional liturgy is threefold. First, in the proper hands, it really does secure practically all the advantages which inhere in the liturgical ways of worship. The optional liturgy is a boon to many a minister. While the service may not pass under this name, which is scarcely ideal, the fact is that in many a church where the Sunday morning hour is uplifting the minister is using an optional liturgy. Without any sense of ecclesiastical compulsion, but rather because he feels led by the Spirit, he uses artistic forms according to his heart's desire. In quest of such forms he may send out a decree that the whole world of sacred art shall be taxed, but in the use of what he gathers from near and far he practices wise restraint. In certain parts of the worship he finds that words of his own choosing can better express the feelings of his friends in the pews. In every part of the hour he plans to do whatever will lead them closest to God.

Such a man of God needs to be an artist. While he can use the fruits of living men's worthy labors, as well as the choicest prayers in the liturgy of any church, including the Catholic, he must use his imagination in knowing when to employ a liturgical prayer and when to phrase one of his own. In any case the decision will depend partly upon his own gifts and limitations, but

71

more largely upon the traditions of the people among whom he ministers. But if he keeps on using his imagination as he prepares to lead in public worship, this highest of human powers will keep on growing, and thus the optional liturgy will become more and more of a means of blessing to the people, as well as a strong factor in the advancement of the Kingdom.

The second reason in favor of the optional liturgy is that it tends to conserve all the advantages of non-liturgical worship. Those advantages are both real and vast. The Church should not let a single one of them disappear from her corporate life. The optional liturgy is in keeping with the ideals of the Scriptures, the best traditions of the Church throughout her history, and the desires of God's people throughout the majority of our churches today.

The third reason is that the optional liturgy opens the way for spiritual adventure, in faith. In a sense, each of the other ways of leading in worship keeps a man looking back, whereas in the wise use of the optional liturgy the minister looks upon the coming hour of worship as a call to follow the Spirit of God in bringing forth from the treasuries of earth and heaven things both new and old. If Charles Silvester Horne had lived a few years longer, he might have delved into the history of the Church and written a book about "The Romance of Christian Worship." If so, as in his book about preaching,[12] he would have shown that every minister who has excelled in the lead-

[12] *The Romance of Preaching*, James Clarke & Co., London, 1914.

ership of worship has done so largely by becoming a pioneer of faith. After a minister has worked at his craft long enough to know his laws, and likewise how to plan a service, he ought to find great joy as he learns how to lead in worship in his own way, but ever for the glory of God.

What a blessed consummation it will be if in these next few years, perhaps under the leadership of our younger ministers, there is a renaissance of this finest of all fine arts. Out of the struggles of the past they will have learned to keep all the forms that are worthy, and then they will go on to use their own God-given powers while leading in worship with a radiance and a power like that of the Apostolic Church.

CHAPTER IV

THE PRACTICAL BEARING OF PSYCHOLOGY

*W*HAT has psychology to do with public worship? That is a mooted question. Surely the first approach should be Biblical, and the second should be historical, but is there any place for the psychological? Dean Willard L. Sperry seems to think that there is little or none.[1] But in this warning, and throughout his noteworthy book, he shows that he himself is familiar with what he rightly fears. So should every minister know something about the teachings of modern psychology, if only for the sake of knowing what to avoid.

Let us think about the psychology of the man in the pew, not of the leader. From this point on we may seem largely to forget about him. Here, then, are five sorts of facts about the normal layman: he is a person with strong native impulses, formerly known as instincts; a set of habits, either good or bad; a certain power of attention, which is closely allied with his interests; a number of sentiments and ideals, the one relating to the present and the other to the future; and a mysterious something known as the unconscious, or the subconscious. In dealing with each of these five facts, the controlling purpose

---

[1] *Reality in Worship,* Macmillan, 1926, p. 170.

is the same: how can one lead such a man in the public worship of God?

THE POWER OF THE NATIVE IMPULSES

Here are certain mental dispositions common to all members of the human species. Opinions differ about the number, the nature, and the cause of these impulses; but practically everyone recognizes that they are at work long before anyone tries to worship God. So let us think about six of them, in pairs, as they concern public worship. Needless to say, there are more than these six.

In the normal man there is a sort of gregarious urge which tends to impel him to seek to be with other people. This is the impulse which should help to bring him to church at the hour of prayer. On the other hand, there is the impulse to fear, with the corresponding tendency toward flight. Fear is perhaps the strongest of these natural forces, except love, which casts out fear. Without the capacity to fear, a man could scarcely worship God with reverence and awe. Instead, therefore, of trying to eradicate or repress this God-given quality, we should try to sublimate it in the spirit of Christian love. That is what we do in worship, especially at the beginning of the hour.

Again, there are the contrasting impulses toward repulsion, or self-abasement, and toward elation, or self-assertion. While these words may not be wholly Christian, they are in common use. Repulsion, or self-abasement, should lead to confession of sin; and elation, or self-assertion, to the outpouring of the soul in song.

75

Once more, the tender emotion, as of a child to a loving father, contrasts with the impulse towards pugnacity. The tender emotion finds expression in the familiar words, "Our Father." (This emotion should be the controlling spirit in all Christian worship.) In fact, the Christian religion at its best is largely the transfiguration of the family. On the other hand, there is a mighty impulse towards combativeness. While Paul was a lover of peace among men, he made constant use of metaphors about war. So should we enlist every layman in the Christian crusade against sin. This is the Christian equivalent of war. Hence there is a place in worship for the martial hymn, such as "The Son of God goes forth to war."

To these impulses, and others like them, the professional evangelist used to appeal in ways which caused many a reverent minister to shake his head. But still it is a question whether any man of God is leading effectively in public worship if he is not somehow appealing to these native impulses. They are ever in the soul, and they seem to be ever at work. Are they to be on the side of God, or of the devil? If on the side of God, how? [2]

In the fifteenth chapter of Luke, for example, these powers are at work; and if one is to read that chapter well, one must by sympathy pass through these shifting experiences of the prodigal son. In like manner, it is good once in a while to glance over the list of hymns, or even the outline for the pastoral prayer, and ask oneself:

[2] See *Human Nature and Its Remaking*, by William E. Hocking, Yale University Press, 1918, pp. 37-83.

76

to which native impulses of the man in the pew will this part of public worship make its appeal? Fortunately, one can pass such an examination after only a modest course of reading in social psychology.

THE IMPORTANCE OF RIGHT HABITS

Another group of psychologists, represented by William James and John Dewey, make more of habit than of impulse. Impulses are innate, or else they emerge soon after birth; habits develop somewhat slowly. Good habits are the foundation of a good life. Such habits are of the essence of public worship. There is reason to believe that habit is the chief factor in bringing many men and women to church. Hence it is essential that the boy and the girl form the right sort of habits. Every leader of public worship should be familiar with the Laws of Habit, as formulated by William James.[3] These are five, all bearing on the principle that we should make automatic and habitual as many useful actions as possible, the earlier in life the better.

First is the injunction to launch oneself with as strong and decided an initiative as possible. When Dean N. S. Shaler went to teach in Harvard, he said that he did not wish to have to decide every morning whether he would attend chapel or not; so he determined to go every day, and he did, for what he used to call his "moral bath." Thus he followed also the second of these laws: "Never suffer an exception to occur until the new habit is firmly

[3] *The Principles of Psychology*, Henry Holt & Co., 1908, I, 104-127.

rooted in your life." From this point of view, the most disheartening fact about church attendance is not the smallness of the numbers, but the irregularity, especially on the part of the boys and girls, as well as the new members. Closely allied to this second law is the third: "Seize the very first opportunity to act on every resolution you make, and on every emotional prompting you may experience in the direction of the habits you aspire to gain."

The fourth law, unlike the others, is addressed to the minister, as the teacher: "Don't preach too much to your pupils, or abound in good talk in the abstract." In other words, it is rarely wise to spend much time in public exhorting children and others to attend public worship. The fifth law, again, is to the worshiper: "Keep the faculty of effort alive in you by a little gratuitous exercise every day." This seems to be the principle on which the Roman Catholics proceed in training boys and girls. As a rule, we Protestants make it seem too easy to be an acceptable member of the church.

Here is an object lesson showing how a busy pastor worked in accordance with these laws, doubtless without intending to do so. In Columbia, S. C., the pastor of the First Baptist Church told a neighboring minister the reason why that place of worship was thronged almost every Sunday night. "When I first came to this parish, the attendance at night was so poor that the officers were losing heart. When I asked them if they wished to keep on holding the evening service, they replied, 'Of course we do! Who ever heard of a Southern Baptist church with no evening service?' So in the fall I got each of them to promise to come to church ahead of time every Sunday evening for six months. With their families they formed a sort of Gideon's band, which largely filled the main floor, and likewise made other people feel at home. Before six months passed, those officers had discovered that the evening service was almost as vital as the one in the morning. If we gave up our evening service once in a while, as the other churches do, we should be educating our people to remain at home. But we must give them something when they come."

These Laws of Habit apply even more directly to the morning service, partly because one is dealing here with boys and girls. If they attend only one service on the Lord's Day, many a minister recommends morning worship. If they form the habit of regular attendance, they are likely to keep on through life. Otherwise, they are likely to drop out of whatever service they attend—usually it is the Bible school—and so they may be lost to the church. But really there is no reason why they should not form the habit of attending both services, with the chief emphasis on morning worship.

So should one encourage the adult to follow these Laws of Habit. When John Timothy Stone was pastor of the Fourth Presbyterian Church in Chicago, he rendered a prominent lawyer a most acceptable service. When the layman thanked him and asked what he could do to show his appreciation, the minister recalled that the lawyer was not a churchgoer. So the request was that he attend the Fourth Church every Sunday morning for six months. The lawyer accepted the invitation, kept his contract; and before the end of the period he united with the church, becoming one of the most useful leaders in that congregation. Though there is no magic virtue about any such ministerial leadership, certainly not in the use of six months as the minimum time limit, surely it is good to deal with every man according to his God-given nature. Good habits rarely come by chance.

THE PSYCHOLOGY OF ATTENTION

Closely allied with the subject of habit is that of attention. Attention itself is a habit, in large measure; but for the sake of emphasis we shall think about attention separately. The word literally means "a being drawn toward" some object, or idea; "a being drawn primarily by forces outside one's self"; that is, the keeping of the mind more or less on a stretch. In other words, attention is an act, not a state. According to the older psychologists, this act may be either voluntary or involuntary. (There is a saying that to one minister's prayers you can listen by an act of the will, oft repeated; to another's you cannot listen, doubtless because he does not know how to pray; and to a third man's prayers you must listen. This sort of involuntary attention is the ideal.)

Attention is the mental activity involved in fixing a certain idea in the center of consciousness, and keeping it there. Perhaps the quickest way for a minister to test

his gifts of leadership in worship is to ascertain his ability
to catch and to hold attention. Psychologically, this
means to "condition the desired response"; that is, to
know the conditions on which attention depends, whether
in an individual or a group, and then to use such knowledge in securing such mental activity. The difficulty is
that attention means mental work, and that many people
have fallen out of the habit of thinking consecutively
about one subject. In view of the modern motion-picture
mind, or lack of mind, the minister must know how to
keep the mental images changing, not fast enough to
make the layman weary, but still fast enough to take
advantage of the "beat" of his mind as it fixes attention
time after time. Is it any wonder that the service sometimes seems wearisome?

These principles apply to almost every aspect of public
worship. For example, think of church architecture.
Experience shows that it is easier to secure the attention
of a layman when the edifice looks like a church, especially if it is the sort of church building which he prefers. Anyone who has ministered in the back alleys of a
city knows that the souls of the poor are being starved
through lack of beauty, and that they wish the place
where they worship to be entirely different from the
hovels where they dwell. Hence the modest chapel
should by its appearance, both without and within, suggest the holiness of beauty. As a rule, we Protestants
set apart for the church too little ground, so that God cannot display his handiwork in the grass, the flowers, and

81

the shrubs. Across the sea, at Hawarden, where Gladstone went to church, or at Stoke Poges, where Thomas Gray wrote his "Elegy Written in a Country Churchyard," we can learn much about the psychology of worship.

One lesson is that the place where people worship should be large enough to accommodate those who come, and not much larger, although it is wise to have provision for an overflow, perhaps in a balcony which is usually kept closed. It is easier to gain and hold the attention of any one person when he is seated in the midst of other people who are paying attention. While there is no virtue in mere numbers, psychology shows the wisdom of having the people sit together, and that not far from the leaders in song and in prayer. Hence the small group worships more fitly in a modest chapel than in a vast cathedral. Such a city as Washington or Pittsburgh needs at least one Gothic edifice to tower above the legislative halls or the marts of trade, reminding busy men that God is first in all human life. In Liverpool two such stately edifices are emerging into grandeur, whereas in Philadelphia or Boston, with all the many churches, there is not one which seems to rise above the city. Nevertheless, the man who has the privilege of leading the worship in a humble sanctuary should daily voice his thanks to God. In a cathedral it might not be easy to keep religion first.

Whatever the architectural plan, the interior appointments should be worshipful. While sojourning in a distant state, a minister walked past a certain church every day and read on the bulletin board an invitation to come in and pray. He wondered why, for the exterior was not inviting, and he never saw any person enter. But one day he did so. Ere long he came out, not having prayed, for there was nothing within to attract his attention towards the things of the Spirit. It would be easier to worship in a barn, provided it looked like a barn. On the other hand, this minister could look back on a prayer meeting attended by twenty-five per cent of the members of the congregation. Those meetings were so satisfactory that he thought he had solved this ever-present problem. But in two other parishes, each larger and more promising, he never again was tempted to be proud of such leadership. The difference was largely in the plan of that first building. It had a room which lent itself admirably to the sort of fireside service which he loved to conduct. Neither of the other church buildings had such equipment, and so the midweek meeting suffered. Perhaps our people ought not to be subject to these influences, due to some person's ignorance of psychology, but facts are facts.

Many a minister wishes that he could help to plan for a new church building, instead of advising with committees about how to raise money to pay for architectural monstrosities erected under his predecessor. But it is possible to make even the least promising structure more worshipful. In time there may be such an architectural transformation as former President J. Ross Stevenson brought about here at Princeton Seminary. A few years ago it was not easy to hold the attention even of theological students when one was leading in worship on the Lord's Day. They preferred to worship almost anywhere rather than in that old chapel with its hybrid architecture and its unseemly appointments. In 1933, through the transfer to another site, the removal of excrescences, and the addition of pleasing appointments, notably the organ, the architect transformed that dumpy meetinghouse into a sanctuary of rare beauty and charm, where the students of architecture at the University spend many an hour tracing the simple lines which help to make it easy to worship God. As a consequence, our students now take delight in the services of this chapel, which in a sense has been saved by grace.

These principles apply, also, to the length of time for the service. Other things being equal, it is easier to hold attention throughout a service which lasts only an hour than during one which holds on for an hour and a half. That is approximately the time it takes for the New York Philharmonic Orchestra to play the *Ninth Symphony* by Beethoven, the longest of his creations. If it were still longer, majestic as it is, the lover of music might grow weary as he followed the interplay of various themes. In that symphony the final movement is unusually long, requiring about thirty minutes. In like manner the exceptional divine can hold the attention throughout a service lasting ninety minutes, with a sermon lasting thirty. But there is a saying that few souls are saved after the first twenty minutes.

Should not this same sort of limitation apply, also, to the other parts of public worship, notably the special music? One professor who was formerly a pastor feels that if he were rejoicing in that privilege now he would keep to sixty minutes, instead of seventy-five, as was his custom. One of our most successful young pastors seems to owe his increasing popularity partly to the fact that he keeps within sixty minutes, and yet he never makes the impression of watching the clock, or of being in haste. While many another minister has the approved idea about brevity, the various parts of the service move along swiftly, like the assembly line in the Ford or the Chevrolet factories at Detroit. Such haste makes for spiritual waste.

During these sixty minutes the leader ought to be able to secure the attention of the worshiper continuously, at each stage helping him to attend to the part of worship then in progress. From this point of view the least worshipful part of the hour is likely to be during the announcements. So why make them? In the Broad Street Presbyterian Church of Columbus, Ohio, which has recently witnessed an architectural transformation, with a renaissance in worship, there are no announcements, and yet everyone is able to follow the service and find the hymns, or the responsive parts, as they come in order. The minister, J. Harry Cotton, says that he is still trying to discover the best ways of filling every minute of the sixty with something that is worthy of attention by the thoughtful lawyer or university professor, as well as by the weary housemother or high school student.

Such a minister thinks a good deal about the bulletin, partly because it goes out through the mail from many homes on Sunday afternoon; and if it is worthy, its leaves are for the healing of souls near and far. But a worthy bulletin who can find? Here is the complaint of a young man who loves to worship in the First Church, near the University, but not in the meetinghouse back at home. "I seldom attend, because I hate the looks of the place, with its unpainted walls, and its unsightly shutters, its slovenly ways of doing the Lord's work, and its lack of reality in public worship. The bulletin last week was mimeographed on cheap, mud-colored paper, with many errors in diction, spelling, and typing. In it was nothing of human interest except the announcement of the 'Pancake Eating Contest,' and the plea to come to church on time, because 'the oily boid gits the wurm.' Why do our people send us away to school to learn to love Milton and Spenser, and then bring us home to worship God in a place less attractive than a barn? The difference is that my father keeps his barn clean."

The obvious reply is that the young man should help to remedy such conditions. For instance, a neat, attractive bulletin costs little more than one which is worse than none. Like many others, the First Presbyterian Church of Berkeley, California, has the bulletin mimeographed. The young woman in charge evidently knows how to make the reading matter contribute to the advancement of the Kingdom, through the local parish, and likewise how to use homemade drawings, on the right sort of paper. When a person enters the sanctuary on Sunday morning and receives a copy of such a bulletin, there is in it nothing to distract his attention, if he is wishing to pray, and everything to attract his attention Godward, if he is inclined to let his attention wander. Yes, it pays to study the psychology of attention.

THE APPEAL TO SENTIMENTS AND IDEALS

More vital than anything thus far in this chapter are the sentiments and ideals. Here the appeal in public worship is usually indirect. Another name for these sentiments is loyalty. In Christian worship, the appeal is for loyalty to home and church, to native land, to world peace, to world-wide missions. Anyone who studies the published sermons of such popular preachers as Clovis G. Chappell and Clarence E. Macartney will notice that, though they differ much from each other, they both appeal for loyalty to God. Doubtless this same element enters largely into all that either of them does in the hour of worship. In a sense, that is what worship is for, to foster and make permanent in the soul of the worshiper the right sort of sentiments; that is, to lead him by God's grace to become loyal to the highest. This truth suggests a working definition of religion. According to Josiah Royce, in a book which many pastors find invaluable, loyalty is "the willing and practical and thoroughgoing devotion of a person to a cause." [4] For the Christian, that cause is the Kingdom, and it is incarnate in Christ.

As for the ideals, they differ from the sentiments as the future differs from the present. The field is the same. The Kingdom of God is both a present reality and a future hope. So the leader of worship should be a practical Christian idealist. For example, there in the third pew from the rear is a young man who is facing more than one of life's great permanent decisions, which are three, though they should be four: "First, whom shall I serve? God or myself? Second, what shall I do? Shall I prepare to teach, or go into business? Third, whom shall I wed? Fourth, where shall we live?" While these questions may not emerge in the pastor's sermon, or even in the prayers, one after another these decisions should come in the experience of the young man who worships aright.

If the leader in worship is a Christian idealist, his spirit of joy and hope will radiate through every part of public worship. The effect upon the boys and girls is even more marked than upon the young people. When Albert Schweitzer was a little boy, he used to go with his father and mother to the house of God, and there his heart was strangely warmed as he saw them reverently engage in the worship of God. Above all was he moved when he saw them commune; for though he was not old enough to understand much that was being said, his little heart responded to God's revelation of himself in the breaking

---

[4] *The Philosophy of Loyalty,* Macmillan, 1908, p. 16.

of the bread. Who has ever reported such an impression made by the sort of "absent treatment" which prevails among our boys and girls on Sunday morning, especially on the high day of the Sacrament? How many of these absentees will find their places some day with Doctor Schweitzer in Africa? [5]

Fortunately, the leadership of a minister who is a Christian idealist appeals to all sorts of people. For instance, when Maltbie D. Babcock was at Brown Memorial Church in Baltimore, there would often be people sitting on the steps leading up to the pulpit. Sometimes the visitor wondered wherein lay the secret of such drawing power. Of course, that leader had what we call charm. But he seems to have known how to use it for the glory of God. As one physician said about those years when he first learned what one means by the romance of worship, "After going to that church for twelve months, I did not know a great deal more, but I was much more determined to be a good and a useful man." Would that the young minister now might learn this same secret of leading in worship, so as to appeal to sentiments and ideals.

THE MYSTERY OF THE UNCONSCIOUS

After dealing with such lofty matters, one hesitates even to refer to the unconscious. This is the sort of subject which one prefers to leave to Freud and Jung. When a little girl was asked to reproduce the sentence,

[5] See *What You Owe Your Child*, by Dean Willard L. Sperry, Harper's, 1935.

THE FINE ART OF PUBLIC WORSHIP

"The cottontail rabbit has no tail to speak of," she wrote, "The cottontail rabbit has a tail, but you mustn't say anything about it." In that case the facts are obvious, but who knows enough to write about the unconscious? However, there is ground for the surmise that this force in every man's soul is as mighty there as gravitation is in the world of matter. What, then, does one mean by the term unconscious? Since usage differs, let us attach a definite meaning to this word, perhaps arbitrarily.

The unconscious is that part of a man's mental life below the horizon of his consciousness. A closely related term is the subconscious. The distinction seems to be that the subconscious has to do with matters which at one time lie below the surface of consciousness and at another time come within the range of one's vision, whereas the unconscious refers to what never comes to the surface. Thus the subconscious is closely related to memory. As an example, for years while Augustine was sowing his wild oats he was scarcely aware of his mother Monica's prayers for him; but when he at last came to himself, he brought those early memories out of their hiding place and made them henceforth a part of his daily consciousness. But if she had died when he was two or three years old, while the impression of her prayers would have been constantly in his soul, they would have been stored away down in the unconscious.[6] For convenience, we shall use this word unconscious as the broad term to include both

[6] Cf. *Christian Nurture*, by Horace Bushnell, Scribner's, 1883, p. 236.

aspects of that inner world of which a man is not aware.

There is reason to believe that this unknown part of a man's personality is more extensive than the known, just as eight-ninths of an iceberg is beneath the surface of the sea. In terms of life about us, the unconscious is like the subsoil which means everything to the growth of the tree. In a sense these unseen forces work best when one leaves them alone, but in another sense they will work best in years to come if one makes upon the soul the right sort of impressions now. That is exactly what one is doing in the leadership of public worship, especially as it concerns young people and children. Not only is one constantly appealing to these unseen elements in the soul of the other person; one is likewise enriching the subsoil, so that in years to come there should be abundance of fruit. But in this mysterious realm, all our figures fall far short of the facts.[7]

Because the unconscious is mighty, it is important to provide the proper sort of atmosphere for public worship. For ten or fifteen minutes before the beginning of the vocal worship there may be quiet, meditative music from the organ. In the lobby the officers should greet those who enter; but in the sanctuary itself everyone should be silent, so as to practice the presence of God. Where such a program is impossible, owing to the need for using the sanctuary as the main room for the Bible school, it is

[7] See The Religious Consciousness, by James B. Pratt, Macmillan, 1928, pp. 45-67.

difficult to create the right sort of atmosphere, but one is more likely to do so if one tries. If there is no pipe organ, it is possible to make good use of the piano. The main thing is to have the will to lead in worship.

Throughout the service, beginning with the prelude, the appeal is largely to the unconscious. This is true especially of the music. Music itself is mystery, and so is the unconscious; hence it is not strange that the one appeals strongly to the other. Albert Einstein said at Princeton University Chapel, when the Philadelphia Symphony and the Westminster Choir College united in rendering Bach's *B Minor Mass,* "Bach is deep!" Later, when he listened to these same singers rendering Handel's *Messiah,* he said, "That is gracious!" Who can ever put into words the effect of such music, especially when it awakens recollections of childhood, and likewise makes one think of the life everlasting?

The same is largely true of prayer. Psychology tells us that when the heart is moved the words tend to flow in a pleasing rhythm. So when the leader is gifted in prayer there is likely to be a corresponding rhythm in the soul of the man in the pew, just as when one bell sounds every other bell near by sounds too if the key is the same. Though the layman is as unconscious of these mental states as the minister ought to be unconscious of how he is feeling while he prays, experience shows that it is easier for the average layman to pray under certain conditions than under others. For example, think of posture. "The bent knee, the closed eye, and other bodily postures com-

92

monly used in worship, have on many a worshiper a decidedly helpful effect in bringing about the religious attitude of mind." [8]   In all these matters the causes lie
largely in the realm of the unknown.

Above all does the power of the unconscious work in
the presence of sacred symbols, such as the Lord's Supper.
This is one reason why many conservative congregations
are restoring the cross to its historic place over the communion table. Otherwise, the table might be used as the
resting place for the collection plates, as well as the altar
flowers. For some reason one never sees flowers in the
baptismal font when it is not being used for its appointed
purpose; why should the communion table seem less sacred? In many a meetinghouse the communion table is
the only one available for use at a congregational meeting, and for other utilitarian purposes. When shall we
learn to take advantage of these silent forces known as
the unconscious?

Largely because of these unseen forces many a humble
child of God keeps on coming to church, though unable
to understand the minister's allusions to Eddington and
Jeans, or to follow the pastoral prayer for the prospective
overthrow of totalitarian despotism. On a Monday morning when such a humble churchgoer was busy with her
week's washing, her parson stopped to "inquire about her
soul." By that he seemed to mean whether or not she
remembered yesterday morning's sermon. When he
learned that she could not recall the text, the topic, or

[8] *The Religious Consciousness,* by J. B. Pratt, Macmillan, 1928, p. 314.

anything that he had said, he asked, "What good does it do you to go to church?"

She replied, "Sir, my soul is like that linen, bleaching in the sun. Every night the dew falls on it, and every morning the linen dries. On a Monday I put it through the wash, and when winter comes again that linen will be whiter than the snow. Can you tell me why?"

"No," said he, "we must leave such a mystery with God."

Thus we have looked in turn at five facts about the inner life of the man in the pew: he has various native impulses; he has a set of habits, more or less firmly fixed; he has certain powers of attention; he has a number of sentiments and ideals; and he has that mysterious something which we call the unconscious. Whether the minister is aware of the fact or not, he appeals to every one of these forces in every hour of public worship. But if he is wise, he never talks to his people in psychological jargon, and he does not make them feel that he is using them as case-studies in pastoral theology. Rather does he wish to be known as a man who loves God, and loves his people, one by one.

When such a minister leads in worship from week to week, he is able to command the respect of those who know a vast deal about psychology. He knows what to do and say, as well as what not to do and say. If in one of the homes a college student says to his mother, "Our minister surely knows his psychology," she will perhaps reply, "Yes, I am sure that he does. For my part, I am glad that he knows the Lord, and that he loves my boy."

CHAPTER V

THE FINE ART OF SACRED MUSIC

MUSIC is the finest of the fine arts, and sacred music ought to be the best of all. Much of it is, for no secular music has ever surpassed the spiritual harmonies of Bach. But in many parishes the minister has to think about church music on a lower level. Sometimes he is tempted to exclaim, "The choir is the war department of the modern church!" Back in the seminary he may have heard a learned professor speak out of vast inexperience as a pastor, "Young man, leave the music alone; mind your own business and preach the Word!" Such teaching may be partly responsible for the low estate of our music. If so, we in the seminaries are ashamed and sorry for our sins of yesterday. We are striving now to aid every former graduate in solving the musical problems of his own parish. The obvious way for him to begin is by working out a sort of homemade philosophy of pastoral leadership in music.

THE PASTOR'S RELATION TO THE MUSIC

In every hour of public worship the pastor is responsible for the music. He selects the hymns. Hence he should enjoy real music and know how to avoid the ama-

95

tory, the sentimental, and the melancholy; or as the wag would say, "the erotic, the exotic, and the tommyrotic." While the minister does not select the music for the prelude or the anthem, he has a good deal to do, indirectly and tactfully, with determining its general character. He may know that the organist and the singers wish to have two heavy anthems every Sunday morning; but, if only for the sake of the boys and girls, he feels that one anthem is enough. When well prepared and well rendered, the inspiring anthem is a decided means of grace. It adds beauty to the hour of worship, and sometimes a touch of splendor. But if poorly chosen and poorly rendered, two anthems would be worse than none.

The minister is responsible, also, for the musical training of the people, especially the young people—the younger the better. His knowledge of psychology strengthens the testimony of the brethren that in the public worship of God the normal boy or girl wishes to be active, not passive; to sing, not to listen; to be dramatic rather than logical. These same principles apply to young people and to many adults, who are only children of a larger growth. Since the best way to get people to sing is to let them sing often, provided they always sing well, the minister makes much of the congregational singing. For example, since the conventional solo by the soprano calls undue attention to one voice, he covets this time for an additional hymn, or else a few musical responses to be sung by the people after the prayers.

Such pastoral leadership in things musical is largely

indirect. It calls for tact and patience. The minister works with the music committee, especially the chairman, who assumes responsibility for every matter of business. Since the peace of the local church is more vital than any improvement in the music, the pastor is careful about suggesting radical changes. In the Gothic chapel of Princeton University he may have witnessed the awesome procession of the Westminster Choir College, with a hundred fifty singers arrayed in "robes of wine and cream." But if he asked for anything of the sort in the modern church at the crossroads, the officers might think that he was beside himself. "Plain horse sense" would tell them that a procession is an orderly way of getting a large group of singers from the robing room into the choir loft without interfering with the devotions of the waiting people. But if there ought to be a procession, sooner or later the people will open up the way with gladness.

Since every parish has its own peculiar needs, the minister and the lay officers, especially the chairman of the music committee, should formulate a definite program. The pastor should encourage them to spend money for the musical training of the young people and the children. In a large parish there should be a children's choir and a junior chorus, a young people's choir and a chorus of adults. Wherever possible there should be a full-time minister of music who will serve as an assistant pastor; but his real work is to train people to sing, not to be the errand boy of the ladies' aid society. If the critics who protest against paying salaries for "highfalutin singers imported from other churches" happen to be Presbyterians, they may not know that unmusical John Calvin sent to France for a layman to teach the people how to sing in church. The results of such expenditures may be slow in appearing, but they are cumulative.

In many parishes, however, such an ambitious program is out of the question. So the minister determines to make the most out of what there is at hand. One way to do that is to cultivate the friendship of the musicians, especially the one in charge. If they are sensitive about their art, they are certain to appreciate personal kindness and intelligent commendation. William P. Merrill, under whose pastoral oversight the music in the Brick Church of New York became worthy of note, tells of a capable organist who worked under a well-known pastor for twelve years with never a word of commendation or thanks, in public or in private. He never spoke to her about the music unless he wished less of it than usual so that he could preach a longer sermon. On the other hand, Frank W. Gunsaulus, of Chicago, used to attend the weekly rehearsals of the choir, not to make suggestions, but to enjoy the musical fellowship. In the smaller parish, too, ministerial thoughtfulness would often pay rich dividends.

THE MINISTER'S KNOWLEDGE OF MUSIC

While he need not be a musician, technically, the minister should know enough about the subject to command the respect of those who know more. Unless he is careful about selecting hymns, for example, he is likely to ask people to march to a tune in three-four time; and then he may wonder why the organist looks on him as an ignoramus. If he succeeds in getting the boys and girls to take a hearty interest in music, he is likely to hear this question, with no time to look up the answer: "In the hymnal what do those letters mean—S.M., C.M., L.M.?"[1] On the other hand, the minister who is reasonably well informed musically, and willing to defer to those who know more, soon gains their respect.[2]

Every pastor should know his church hymnal better than any other book except the Bible. One way to become acquainted with an unfamiliar hymnal quickly is to sing through it with one's wife at the piano, marking each song for speedy reference. A cross might indicate that the tune is familiar; a cipher, that it is probably beyond the present capacity of the people; another mark, such as "L," that this is a good song for them to learn. Through the file of past bulletins, and through the organist and others with musical taste, one may ascertain which tunes are familiar to the people. For his own guidance, the minister may jot down on the margin from week to week a few hieroglyphics, such as "A.M. 3-'39" or "P.M. 12-'39," to indicate how often, and when, he

---

[1] These abbreviations indicate the number of syllables to the line; short meter is 6, 6, 8, 6; common meter, 8, 6, 8, 6; long meter, 8, 8, 8, 8. See *The Hymn as Literature*, by Jeremiah B. Reeves, Century, 1924, pp. 34, 35.

[2] See *Church Music and Worship*, by Earl E. Harper, Abingdon, 1924. pp. 61-81, *et al.*

has called for "Guide me, O thou great Jehovah." As in coming to know the Bible, the obvious way to master the hymnbook is to use it every day, each time with a definite aim. Soon the heart learns to love such daily food.

Since the minister is a home missionary of music, he ought to know what his people like and what they do not like. In a parish with a large resident membership and a large student constituency, the pastor requested the older people to hand in lists of their favorite hymns, without specifying any number, and the assistant pastor secured similar lists from the young people. In each group the response was gratifying, for those people loved to sing in church. The two lists appear below. In each column the most popular hymn is first, and the least popular is last. A glance over the two lists will show that each in its way is practically as good as the other, and that only one hymn appears in both. This is "How firm a foundation." Henry van Dyke used to say that this is the hymn which the average congregation sings better than any other in the book.

Rock of Ages	Holy, holy, holy
Abide with me	There is a green hill
Jesus, Lover of my soul	For the beauty of the earth
Nearer, my God, to thee	Onward, Christian soldiers
Lead, kindly Light	Stand up, stand up for Jesus
How firm a foundation	I love to tell the story
What a Friend	How firm a foundation
Sweet hour of prayer	Lead on, O King Eternal

The Lord's my Shepherd	O come, all ye faithful
When I survey	Christ, the Lord, is risen
Come, Thou Almighty King	America, the beautiful
	Kipling's Recessional
O could I speak	

Many of the mature folk gave the first place to the hymn which they had sung in the presence of death. They had gone through the deep waters, and had learned to love the sort of song which would bring them close to the heart of God. They associated all these hymns with thoughts of mother, home, and heaven. The choice shows a decided preference for the individual, not the social Gospel. Here are simple, old-fashioned songs about Christ and the Cross, the forgiveness of sins, and the life everlasting. Such hymns remind us that in the New Testament the center of gravity is beyond the grave.

It used to seem smart to sneer at such "otherworldliness"; but with advancing years some of us have learned that many a strong man comes to church partly because he wishes to be sure about the life everlasting, and that the best answer to his unspoken question is often in the hymns and the prayers rather than in the sermon. So does he wish to be sure about the forgiveness of sins; here again the answer often comes best in the old-time hymns. In a striking utterance, Bishop Edwin H. Hughes says of *The Methodist Hymnal,* which is second to none of its kind: " 'The Gospel' section was increased until the number equaled seventy-one. Of all these hymns,

101

changes in methodist evangelism

not one was written in this twentieth century. . . . Is there significance in the fact that no hymn of invitation to come to Christ, as selected for 'The Gospel' section, was pulled from an author's heart in the last forty years?" [3] Of these seventy-one hymns twenty-nine were written before 1800 A.D., and the others during the nineteenth century. Twelve are by Charles Wesley, whose hymns some of us love best of all.

old people like

As a rule, then, among the various denominations the older people prefer the older hymns. In that list of twelve selected by Presbyterian older folk, every one is in *The Methodist Hymnal,* issued in 1935; and all but one are in *The Hymnal* issued by the Presbyterian Church, U. S. A., in 1933. Some of our Presbyterian older people are asking why our Hymnal does not include "Sweet hour of prayer" and other old-fashioned songs which the Methodists are still singing. Whether the minister sympathizes or not, he should surely take such feelings into account when he plans for public worship. If he wishes at night to appeal to a group somewhat older and more thoughtful than in the morning, he should confine the hymns largely to the sort which the older people love.

young people like

A glance over the other list will show that the young people prefer a greater variety of hymns, old as well as new. They love songs of joy, with stirring action, emphasis on the present rather than the future, inspiration rather than comfort, and the call to social service as well as to

[3] *Evangelism and Change,* Methodist Book Concern, 1938, p. 11.

individual aspiration. As a rule these young people seem to be more concerned about the tune than about the words. With few exceptions they chose the better popular tunes, but no better, perhaps, than those on the other list.

In the light of such facts, how shall the minister "turn the heart of the fathers to the children, and the heart of the children to their fathers"? Without calling attention to the widening gulf between the old and the young, the minister can help the older folk to see the beauty of the hymns which the young people prefer, and the young folk to enter into the spirit of the other songs. Lovingly one ought to prepare the young people for dark days, sure to come. Of the twelve hymns on that second list, only two would bring peace amid the shadows of the dark valley. Those young people did not even select "When I survey the wondrous cross," which Matthew Arnold and other noteworthy critics of world literature have declared to be the noblest English hymn. During the World War, according to John Kelman, of Edinburgh, who spent much of his time with the young men at the front, this was their favorite hymn. Even in days of peace one ought to help them make ready for the time when they will be no longer young and free from sorrow.

THE USE OF HYMNS IN PREACHING

One of the surest ways to become an effective home missionary of music is to use the hymnal as a source book for one's sermons. Here is an unfailing source of illustrations. Since many a worthy hymn is taken from the Scriptures, the easiest way to throw a pleasing light upon many a passage is to refer to the hymn which embodies the same aspect of the truth about God. "Nearer, my God, to Thee," for example, throws light upon the experience of Jacob at Bethel. "Lead on, O King Eternal" belongs with a sermon about the Children of Israel as they were preparing to cross the Red Sea. Any minister who wishes to combine his reading of the Scriptures with his mastery of the hymnal should make a list showing the passages which he finds reflected in the various hymns. Such a list keeps on growing through the years.

More direct is the plan of using a hymn as the basis for a doctrinal sermon, though one need not call it by that name. Instead of trying to explain and define the mystery of the Trinity, one need only take up the hymn, "Holy, holy, holy," and point out what it says about "God in three persons, blessed Trinity." While the mystery will remain, it will seem more than ever a mystery of light. Much easier to handle in this way is "Come, Thou Almighty King," for the first stanza is about God the Father; the second, God the Son; the third, God the Spirit; and the fourth, the "Great One in Three." Especially when these are the first two hymns in the book, what an introduction to the most Christian of all our books except the Bible! Equally satisfying is a sermon from "There is a green hill far away," with the subject, "Why did Jesus die?" While Mrs. Cecil F. Alexander

104

wrote this hymn for boys and girls, it is one of the favorites among many older people.

Such an occasional sermon proves so effective that one often wishes to prepare a brief series. In a certain parish the bulletin during November contained a list of fifteen Christmas songs, the fifteen which the boys and girls from the public schools sang each year in the city auditorium. The minister requested each person to check the four songs which he loved best and then hand in the sheet. A hundred ten persons complied, representing almost a hundred different homes. On four successive Sunday evenings, closing on the one before New Year's Day, the minister preached about "The Gospel Message of the Christmas Hymns," using topics based on the four hymns which the people selected, as follows:

"O come, all ye faithful"—"The Christmas Call to Worship"

"O little town of Bethlehem"—"The Quietness of True Religion"

"Hark! the herald angels sing"—"The Kingship of Christ"

"Joy to the world"—"The Afterglow of Christmas"

In the sermon which grew out of the greatest of all our Christmas hymns, "Hark! the herald angels sing," he showed how the words of Charles Wesley voice almost every glorious truth about the Lord Jesus Christ. Since the robust song by Isaac Watts, "Joy to the world," contains not a single word about Christmas itself, he found this song especially fitting to inspire the members of his congregation as they faced the beginning of a new year. Each of the messages, notably the last, was largely evangelistic, thus leading up to the communion service in January.

In a community where the people were supposed not to be willing to worship in public after the noon dinner on the Lord's Day, the attendance at those evening meetings was good at the start; and it kept growing from night to night. The permanent effect upon the evening worship was gratifying, and so was the increased attention to the spiritual meaning of hymns. This is one way of preaching with the people, instead of merely to them as passive hearers.

After people have enjoyed such a series, they will wish something more of the same kind. At the midweek meeting one can devote an evening to the study of a hymn, such as "Rock of Ages." Better still, one can devote four or five successive Wednesday evenings to hymns by Isaac Watts, and a year later a similar period to those of Charles Wesley. At the first meeting, for example, one might have the people sing a number of Wesley's best-known songs, and then tell them informally about his spiritual experience, devoting the next three popular studies, in turn, to "Jesus, Lover of my soul, "O for a thousand tongues," and "Love divine, all loves excelling." Charles Wesley wrote the first of these songs in 1740, and the second in 1739. Here is a hint for 1939 and 1940.

In short, the pastor's relation to the music is that of

leadership, largely indirect. In the conduct of public worship he calls no attention to how he is leading; elsewhere he makes no show of authority. He becomes increasingly familiar with church music, making it a lifelong study, and he looks upon his hymnal as a sort of musical Bible. He cultivates the fine art of getting along with the lay leaders of music and with the members of the committee, working with them, not over them. He knows the heart needs of the friends who sit in the pews as the shepherd knows his sheep, and he loves to lead the people into the enjoyment of the music that will do them the most good. Best of all, he knows the Lord and finds in prayer the way to solve every problem as it arises.

As a noteworthy example of such leadership, take the pastor of the Emory Methodist Episcopal Church in Pittsburg, Warren W. Wiant. On a Sunday evening in 1938, in a district where attendance at evening worship had almost reached the vanishing point, he welcomed 1,175 persons, who came out to enjoy the rich old hymns. The correspondent quotes him as saying, "It is the part of wisdom for the church to invest money in the musical ability of its own people." [4] Doubtless he has likewise invested a vast deal of time and thought, as well as prayer. How else could a minister expect to have a revival of music in the local parish?

The results of such pastoral leadership and teaching may appear gradually, but they abide. When the min-

[4] *The Christian Century*, May 18, 1938, p. 633.

ister moves to another field, the organist thanks him privately for making her ministry a source of increasing joy, and the people thank him publicly for teaching them to love the noblest hymns. Under his successor, they may carry out the program of having a full-time "minister of music," who will train the people to sing with the spirit and the understanding. No longer will the boys wish to hie away to Trinity Episcopal Church, so as to be able to sing with men. Thus will the congregation make more and more of its music as one of the most beautiful gifts of God to men. Here, then, is the pastor's ideal for transforming a troublesome problem into an attractive opportunity for service.

In music, as in everything else, the Christian minister should be a practical idealist. So he should think of the place of worship as the sanctuary. Some day perhaps he will visit the Bird Sanctuary at the Bok Memorial Tower in Florida. There, amid the trees and the music of the birds, he will find a modest board with an inscription borrowed from John Burroughs—an inscription which shows why many a strong man or weary woman comes to church and enjoys the music.

> I come here to find myself;
> it is so easy to get lost
> in the world.

CHAPTER VI

THE ART OF SELECTING THE HYMNS

ON any Lord's Day the helpfulness of the congregational singing depends largely upon the selection of the hymns. Every hymnal contains at least a hundred songs which the people should be able to sing with ease and joy. Since not all these songs are of equal value, the minister should know how to select those which will best meet the needs of the hour. Likewise, he should be able gradually to increase the congregational repertoire of worthy hymns. Fortunately, he need not experiment, for the experience of the Church has afforded an exacting proving ground. Out of that age-long experience have come three simple tests of a hymn and four practical tests of a hymn tune. Since the words are more vital than the tune, we shall begin with the tests of the subject matter.

THREE TESTS OF A HYMN

First, is the content Christian? Is the substance biblical? While the hymn should be devotional, not didactic, it should embody Christian truth set to music. The seventy-one hymns about which Bishop Hughes writes[1]

[1] See page 101.

are dear to the Christian heart because they are saturated with the spirit of the Book; some of the more recent hymns are not so dear because they are not so biblical. According to the father of modern hymnody, Isaac Watts, a Christian hymn is the singer's response to God's revelation of himself in Jesus Christ. In writing more than six thousand hymns Charles Wesley held to the same high standard. So did Henry van Dyke when he composed "Joyful, joyful, we adore thee." [2] But not all our recent hymns are able to pass this first searching test. As a rule the old songs are the best.

Many of our noblest hymns are from the Book of Psalms. "Jesus shall reign where'er the sun" is a modern version of the seventy-second psalm, and "Our God, our help in ages past" is a paraphrase of the ninetieth. In the United Presbyterian book of praise are a hundred fifty selections from the Psalms, with an equal number of classic hymns. Perhaps our other denominations would have greater love for the Bible if we sang from the Psalms as often as our fathers did after the Reformation. Many of those songs came out of the fiery furnace, and so they brought our fathers a mighty sense of God's holiness, as well as a keen awareness of his laws. During the War of 1861-65 a wholesale house in Cincinnati sent a representative out over Ohio to collect bills long overdue. In a few days he returned and reported that he could scarcely secure money enough to meet his traveling ex-

[2] This hymn owes its widespread favor partly to the music, the "Hymn to Joy," from the fourth movement of Beethoven's *Ninth Symphony*.

penses. "Everywhere else I get nothing save promises, but up in Xenia those United Presbyterians are singing the Psalms of David and paying down a hundred cents on the dollar." Yes, our songs of praise should be biblical.

Second, is the spirit of this hymn worshipful? Does it express Christian feeling, or does it merely impress Christian doctrine? Is it a Christian lyric, or simply a little sermon set to music? For example, the "Crusader's Hymn"—"Fairest Lord Jesus"—is surely a lyric worthy to appear in any anthology. So is the hymn written by Harry W. Farrington in 1910, "I know not how that Bethlehem's Babe could in the Godhead be." On the other hand, does the didactic hymn, "Prayer is the soul's sincere desire, unuttered or expressed"—at least in the first five stanzas—ever move a man to fall upon his knees? In our modern books of praise, however, this sort of didactic hymn is rare, so rare that the minister may not be able to find three hymns bearing directly on the subject of his next sermon. If so, he may thank God, and give the preference to hymns that are worshipful.

Ordinarily, the spirit of the hymn should be joyful, not disconsolate. The people have troubles enough already, without finding more when they come to church. Partly because it is depressing, that noble piece of Latin verse, "Dies Irae"—"Day of wrath, O day of mourning"—has been dropped from recent hymnals. But still in many a congregation there is too much music that is melancholy. Bad as it is when the minister feels called to preach as "a loquacious apostle of sweetness and darkness," it is dou-

111

bly bad if he keeps the people singing, "Art thou weary, art thou troubled, art thou sore distressed?" and "The sands of time are sinking." Doubtless there should be a place for such songs, but surely that place is small. Far more likely to meet the needs of the hour, especially when times are hard, is such a robust, masculine hymn as "Now thank we all our God." With our Lutheran friends, all of us Christians ought to keep sounding the two distinctive notes of our holy faith, forgiveness of sins and joy in the Lord. If at times the joy seems remote from the experience of the man in the pew, such a song as "Jerusalem the Golden" should encourage him to keep looking and reaching up. As Browning says, "A man's reach should exceed his grasp, or what's a heaven for?"

Third, is the style lyrical? [3] Does the hymn appeal to the imagination, with words which help a man to see, to feel, to move? Or is it only a piece of doggerel verse? While the hymn may not be one of the world's classic poems, it should move in a realm of beauty, and likewise lend itself to singing. The writing of a real hymn calls for ability of a high order. Not long before Lord Tennyson died, he told the President of Magdalen College, Oxford, "A good hymn is the most difficult thing in the world to write. The moment you cease to be commonplace, and put in any expression at all out of the common, it ceases to be a hymn."

[3] Cf. *The Hymnody of the Christian Church*, by Louis F. Benson, Doran, 1927, pp. 99-138.

If being commonplace were the chief essential, many a modern effort could qualify as a first-class hymn. But Lord Tennyson takes for granted that such a sacred song has a quiet beauty all its own. Beauty is no substitute for spiritual content or the worshipful quality. In fact our third test of a hymn is much like the second. In a worthy hymn, as in a good woman, character is first, personality is second, and dress is third. The three belong together, and so one judges the hymn as a whole. If it lives on after the conditions which produced it have passed away, it must have solid worth. For instance, George Matheson's hymn, "O love that wilt not let me go," embodies Christian feeling clothed in a garment of beautiful words. For a still loftier example of Christian sentiment voiced in a Christian spirit and clothed in a worthy style, think of Matthew Bridges's "Crown him with many crowns."

FOUR TESTS OF A HYMN TUNE

The popular favor of a hymn often depends more upon the tune than upon the words. As sons and daughters of the Reformation some of us feel that the words are more vital, but our sons and daughters are becoming so embued with the spirit of the Renaissance that they are demanding better tunes. Thus far many of our hymns have been worthy of better music, but that does not seem to be the case in the most recent church hymnals. Even there, however, the music may represent a compromise between the desires of the experts and the demands of the people. Surely the people ought to have more light.

113

When they ask the minister why the new church hymnal gives the preference to a certain tune, he ought to be able to talk about the subject. He may even explain these four practical tests of a hymn tune.

First, is it worshipful? Are the suggestions devotional? Is the connotation, or "tone color," Christian? This test is largely a matter of personal opinion, and opinions differ; but when the experts agree that a certain tune is sacred or secular, it is wise to accept their appraisal. They tell us that the devotional value of a tune depends largely upon its associations.[4] Even the most sacred music is not so in itself, but it becomes so by use. The issue seems to depend largely upon whether the Church or the world first captures the tune. While many a melody in three-four time has associations which are wholly religious, music of this sort is likely to suggest dancing, and that not before the Lord. For an example, take the lilting tune, "Galilee," to which we often sing those precious words, "Jesus calls us, o'er the tumult of our life's wild, restless sea."

Association, however, can be secular without being sinful. While singing Whittier's hymn, "Immortal love, forever full" ("We may not climb the heavenly steeps"), set to the tune "Serenity," someone may recognize the tune as part of a light opera by William V. Wallace. Everyone likes to sing "Old Black Joe," but one hesitates

---

[4] For an entertaining account of these matters read *The Common Sense of Music*, by Sigmund G. Spaeth, Garden City Pub. Co., 1936 For a treatment by a master of sacred music see *Protestant Church Music in America*, by Archibald T. Davison, E. C. Schirmer Co., 1933.

to use this melody with words about Jesus, as is sometimes done in the Salvation Army. In its proper setting
we enjoy the "Sextet" from *Lucia,* but not when sung in
church by a mixed quartet. On the other hand, we never
grow weary of the "Hallelujah Chorus" from *The Messiah,* when properly rendered; and we do not love the
music less because it has been parodied in "Yes, we have
no bananas." Where the original association is religious
and pleasurable, counter impressions only strengthen our
first love.

Second, is the tune adapted to the words? Not every
melody marked C.M.D. fits every hymn written in that
meter; but when Horatius Bonar's hymn, "I heard the
voice of Jesus say," is sung to Dykes's tune, "Vox Dilecti,"
there is an ideal wedding of music and words. At the
middle of each stanza the mood of wistful seeking gives
way before the spirit of joyful finding, and so the melody
shifts from the minor to the major. Since the helpfulness
of church music depends largely upon the associations
which it revives, the older people prefer to sing "All hail
the power of Jesus' name" to "Coronation," and "For all
the saints, who from their labors rest" to "Sarum." But
the young people, who cherish no such hallowed memories, are more likely to prefer "Miles Lane" to "Coronation," and Vaughan Williams's "Sine Nomine" to Barnby's "Sarum." In both cases, the young people are in
accord with the experts.

Third, is the tune adapted to congregational singing?
As a rule, the best music for this purpose is simple. One

115

reason why Watts's hymn, "Our God, our help in ages past," is one of the most beloved in the book is because of the sturdy old tune, "Saint Anne." In another of the psalm-tunes, "Old Hundredth," both the soprano and the bass keep within the octave. But in "Armageddon," the accepted tune for "Who is on the Lord's side?" both the soprano and the bass must have a range of ten notes. There is a growing feeling that the congregational singing would be better if everyone sang in unison; but even so, the experts who compile the hymnal as a labor of love sometimes forget that the man in the pew is neither a Chaliapin nor a Lawrence Tibbett. Fortunately, every church hymnal contains a large number of tunes which pass this third test, as well as all the others.

Fourth, is the tune acceptable to the musicians? At the Westminster Choir College they tell us that some of our American hymn tunes are good, and that many are not. Among the well-known American composers are Hastings and Lowell Mason, Bradbury and Webb, Doane and Woodbury, with Horatio W. Parker more by himself, and often on a higher level. These American tunes are easy to sing, because they rely largely upon rhythm. Partly because we have used many of these American tunes, our church music has seldom met with favor among the critics.

As a rule, the English tunes of the nineteenth century are better, because they depend more largely upon melody. The mid-Victorian composers include Dykes and Barnby, Elvey and Goss, Smart and Monk, with Sullivan largely by himself In recent years the work of these men has been under fire. Barnby, in particular, has been the butt of scathing criticisms, because some of his melodies have a cloying sweetness; and Sullivan, because many of his tunes have a martial swing. The fact remains that in many congregations the minister is delighted if his people love to sing these mid-Victorian tunes, such as Barnby's "Laudes Domini"—"When morning gilds the skies."

Best of all are the older tunes. Without exception they come from across the sea. Most triumphantly have they stood the test of time. Here are old Psalm tunes, such as "Dundee," which appears with three hymns in the latest Presbyterian book, and with five in the still later book of the Methodists; rich old German chorales, such as Haydn's "Austria"—"Glorious things of thee are spoken"—and Luther's "Ein' Feste Burg"—"A mighty fortress is our God"; traditional melodies from England and Wales, Germany and France; and stately music from the Roman Church before the Reformation. For example, "Veni Emmanuel"—"O come, O come, Emmanuel"—hails from the twelfth century; and "Saint Andrew of Crete"—"Christian! dost thou see them?"—harks from the early Middle Ages. However, according to the common people, some of these majestic tunes, such as the "Passion Chorale"—"O sacred head, now wounded"—are not easy to sing. This is partly due to the fact that they depend chiefly upon harmony.

Broadly speaking, childlike people love rhythm; many of the common people have learned to enjoy melody;

117

real musicians also insist upon harmony. (In terms of popular psychology, rhythm appeals to the instincts, melody to the emotions, harmony to the intellect.) For example, think of the old-fashioned fife and drum corps, with its strongly accented rhythm, which any boy's feet could follow. Think of a social gathering where every person joins in singing "The Bells of Saint Mary's," with a melody which almost sings itself. Think of the Philadelphia Symphony Orchestra rendering Bach's *B Minor Mass,* with its exquisite harmony. In a certain parish, the majority of the people like the Lowell Mason kind of rhythm, if not the Moody and Sankey songs; the more discriminating prefer the Dykes sort of melody; the select few, including the minister and his wife, enjoy the Bach type of harmony.

Never in a single generation has any country witnessed such an advance in musical appreciation as some of us have watched since 1903, when David R. Breed first sent out his book.[5] In that day the majority of his ministerial readers probably preferred the Lowell Mason kind of rhythm, if not the gospel songs, whereas Breed himself strongly advocated the Dykes sort of melody. Many whom he influenced are now thinking in terms of Bach. But the advance has not been uniform. In almost every parish there are people who wonder why the new church hymnal does not include "The old rugged cross." Sometimes they suspect that it is missing because of its strong

[5] *The History and Use of Hymns and Hymn Tunes,* Revell (latest edition, 1934).

evangelical flavor, but the minister knows that this hymn can scarcely pass the three tests stated above, and that the tune cannot pass these four tests of musical excellence. In view of such a conflict between the musical idealism of the few and the lower standards of the many, what should the minister do? This question leads us to consider briefly the gospel songs.[6]

The present tendency is away from what the critics call "the I and me hymns," "the weary Willie songs," and "the self-centered egotism of the Glory Song." But surely that is going too far. The wise minister never voices any criticism of a hymn or a tune which other people love. He knows that there is a place for the gospel songs. Of the seventy-one hymns listed under "The Gospel" in *The Methodist Hymnal*, almost one half would be counted gospel songs. Some of us who admire the Presbyterian *Hymnal* for its high musical standards feel that it would be better adapted for use in many modest chapels if there were more of these songs, such as "O happy day, that fixed my choice" and "Holy Spirit, faithful Guide." It is a wise rule to take the people as one finds them and gradually lead them up to something better.

THE INTRODUCTION OF NEW HYMNS

Many a minister can think of beautiful, uplifting hymns which he hesitates to use lest they fall flat. In the average

[6] For a sympathetic treatment see *Church Music,* by Edmund S. Lorenz, Revell, 1923, pp. 303-352; for the other side see *Practical Hymnology,* by Hubert M. Poteat, Gorham Press, Boston, 1921, pp. 56-94.

parish the repertoire is limited; it is sometimes less than fifty, and only half of these may be hymns of the first order. If the minister could lead the people in learning to sing fifty others, there would be three times as many first-class hymns. But if he asked them to learn that many new songs, or even half that many, he would defeat his own purpose. It is possible, however, in a few years largely to transform the music of almost any congregation which is backward in this respect—and that without arousing opposition.

The best place to begin is with the boys and girls. In a congregation where the Bible school and the Christian Endeavor societies used a gospel songbook not published by a reputable firm, the officers waited until the flimsy books began to fall to pieces, and then quietly introduced *The Hymnal for American Youth,* by H. Augustine Smith. In a few years the younger members of the congregation had practically ceased to care for the brass band tune wedded to a sickly sentiment and clad in tawdry verse. One lad, five years of age, used to talk about his favorite hymns: "Joy to the world," "We three kings of Orient are," and "Lead on, O King Eternal." Now that he is a man, he gives the first place to the creations of Bach, Beethoven, and Wagner; but there is still room for those melodies which were dear in boyhood.

In choosing the hymns from week to week the minister keeps ever in mind these little ones whom he wishes to see in church on Sunday morning. Boys and girls are more likely to be present if they know that there will be

120

at least one hymn which they can sing gloriously. The special hymn may not be a juvenile song, for it is good to keep them reaching up, though never far. Often we underestimate the possibilities of our children. One day a pastor requested each pupil in his class in turn to mention a favorite hymn. The first to respond was a girl ten years of age, who said that the song she loved best was, "I heard the voice of Jesus say." That is not a "children's hymn," but it was one that she had been singing for three or four successive Sunday mornings in church, and between times at her home.

In dealing with the older people, one ought to work more slowly. First of all, one may draw up a list of about fifty hymns, and then plan to introduce ten or twelve each year, thus supplementing those already in frequent use. One congregation may need to learn "Where cross the crowded ways of life"—"Germany"— whereas another may need to know "All glory, laud, and honor"—"Saint Theoldulph." Instead of announcing that the people must master ten or twelve unfamiliar tunes, each of which may seem formidable, one quietly begins with such an attractive song as "Now thank we all our God"—"Nun Danket"—stressing the words. One explains the matter carefully to the leader of the choir, and suggests that she use this hymn as a voluntary, training the singers so that they will make it shine.

It is wise also to enlist the aid of certain other people, such as those who attend the midweek service. There the leader can explain the matter, have the friends sing

121

the unfamiliar song once or twice, and then ask them to sing it in their homes. If he is tactful, he can persuade a number of his people to secure copies of the church hymnal from their denominational bookstore. Ere long, when the "new hymn" finds its way into the morning service, these people will look upon it as a friend. Thus there will be nothing to detract from the spirit of worship. In the holiest hour of all the week, there is no time or need for drilling the people in sacred music, or anything else. While the leader may have been thinking much about that troublesome word, "How?" the people will worship better if they can forget that they are singing the "new hymn" for the first time in the church.

In presenting the unfamiliar song, the order of service may refer to it as a "memory hymn," or a "hymn for boys and girls." In another part of the the bulletin there may be a few words about the words and the author. A week later, this same hymn should appear again in the order of service, and remain there until the people can sing it with ease and power. Then it should give place to another song of a different kind, such as "Praise to the Lord, the Almighty, the King of creation!" with the tune, "Lobe Den Herren," for which the pastor has been quietly preparing the way.

In such leadership he does well to employ Thorndike's three Laws of Learning.[7] The Law of Readiness is that

[7] *The Psychology of Learning,* by Edward L. Thorndike, Columbia University Press, 1913, pp. 1-5.

when a person is ready to act in a certain way, for him to act in that way is satisfying. (In other words, prepare - 1. the way before you announce the unfamiliar song.) The Law of Effect is that when a person acts in a certain way, and the action is satisfying, he is likely to repeat the action. (Introduce only the song which is reasonably sure to give - 2 - satisfaction the first time; then use this same song again.) The Law of Exercise is that when a person repeats an action which satisfies some real want, such a way of action tends to become a habit. (Help the layman to form - 3 - the habit of using in worship the hymn that is worth while.) Undergirding these precepts is the Law of Love, as it applies to the hymn and the people. When the minister loves his people and his hymnal, he finds satisfaction in leading the people to love the hymnal.

The application should be obvious. One prepares the way before one announces the unfamiliar hymn, thus leading the people to look forward with pleasant anticipations. One takes advantage of the desire to repeat the hymn which has brought satisfaction, partly because of the joy of achievement, but more because the hymn voices the unspoken feelings of many a heart. While the difficulty is in learning the tune, the value is largely in voicing the words. So one keeps on using the hymn in public worship, as often as the guiding purpose suggests. All the while one remembers that in each of his laws Thorndike makes room for the baleful effects wrought by acting at the wrong time or in the wrong way. In other words, the minister should choose the hymns which best meet the needs of his people now, and not try to make them conform to arbitrary ideas.

THE CHOICE OF HYMNS FOR NEXT SUNDAY

The real test of these principles comes when a man sits down to choose six or seven hymns, each for a different purpose. Since the best way to promote congregational singing is to have the people sing, provided they sing well each time, he prefers to have three hymns rather than two at morning worship, and a varying number in the evening, but seldom fewer than three or four. Since each of these services should differ from the other, and thus make its own distinctive appeal, so should the two lists of hymns be somewhat different. If in the morning a man wishes to attract the young people, as well as the boys and girls, he will incline towards hymns that appeal to them. If he wishes especially to attract the young people at night, he will plan some other sort of service for the earlier hour. In short, while each man should choose the hymns in his own way, everyone should do so in accordance with his plan for the hour.

Let us think about the hymns for a typical Sunday morning service. Since the chief purpose of the hour is to bring the people, one by one, into right relations with God, and thus enable them to worship him, the first song should be somewhat objective. "Holy, holy, holy!" is admirable, and so is "O worship the King." Many of these objective hymns are in the first few sections of the book, but others appear elsewhere; for example, "Crown

124

him with many crowns." Any such hymn early in the service, if the people sing it well, gives the entire hour a sense of uplift, which might be lacking if they started out by singing. "Stand up, stand up for Jesus." Since man's chief end is to glorify God, it is good to begin public worship with a song about him. "First things first!"

The second hymn may be more of a blending of the objective and the subjective. As an example, take Charles Wesley's, "Love divine, all loves excelling." It is so nearly ideal, especially near the middle of the hour, that one uses this hymn again and again. Such a song helps to prepare the way for many a sermon about the Saviour. When the hymn comes immediately before the sermon, as is often the case, the one provides the background for the other, and likewise suggests much of the atmosphere, but without unduly anticipating what the minister is to say. For instance, at the Brick Church of New York, on a Sunday morning shortly after Easter, William P. Merrill was preaching about "Loyalty to the Highest." [8] The first hymn was "Holy, holy, holy!" thus bringing the people consciously into the presence of God. The second hymn was Maltbie D. Babcock's, "This is my Father's world." A study of this hymn, with the text and the topic, will show how an artist lovingly plans such details.

When there is a closing hymn, it is usually subjective. In the entire service, there is no other place where the man in the pew should be so sure to feel like exclaiming, with young Isaiah in the Temple, "Here am I; send me!"

[8] I John 5:21.

While some of the theorists about worship would have us practically eliminate all use of the words "I" and "me," these words still appear on practically every page in the Psalms, as well as in any worthy hymnal. In the heart of the layman at worship, while God should ever be first, and the people among whom he lives should not long be out of his mind, this closing hymn justifies itself most surely when it expresses his desire to dedicate himself to Christian service, and to do so now. For example, take Washington Gladden's hymn, "O Master, let me walk with Thee."

The list of the hymns should go to the leader of the music early in the week. With it should go everything that she ought to have in mind in choosing the special music. Better still is a personal conference, in which the minister explains what he has in mind for each part of the service, especially the hymns, and keeps himself open for suggestions. If it seems necessary to ask that in the hymn, "When I survey the wondrous cross," the choir and the people should sing the third stanza softly, it is better to make the request verbally, and in private. But whenever one wishes to say anything pleasant, it is good to say it to the group, or else to write it down and send it by mail. Years later, when the organist has died and her friends go through her papers, they will find more than one loving message from her pastor. For example, he writes to thank her for playing the hymns deliberately and with a decided beat.

A glance back over this chapter will show that, although

the selection of the hymns for any one service may seem like a simple undertaking, the expenditure of time and thought will prove rewarding. After a man learns how to do this sort of work, by doing it week after week, he finds that there is as much sheer delight in selecting hymns as there is in a round of golf. He comes to know a good hymn as soon as he sees it, and to size up any new tune when he hears it well sung. He learns how to bring forth from his treasure house things new and old, with increasing delight in the old. And he learns how to select exactly the song which the people will need at a certain place in the service next Sunday morning. In short, the fine art of selecting hymns affords the minister an opportunity to school himself, while he is training the people to love the highest in church music.

4 tests for a

P. 113 Hymn Tune

P. 109 3 tests for Hymn Verse

Plus ways to introduce new hymns

3 Kinds of hymns for morning service
1. obj. 2. inter. 3. sub.

CHAPTER VII

THE PUBLIC READING OF
THE SCRIPTURES

*T*HE reading of the Scriptures is perhaps the most important part of public worship. When James Black was preparing to lecture at Union Seminary, in Richmond, Virginia, he asked a number of thoughtful laymen what he should say, and practically every one of them advised him to stress the reading of the Scriptures. He said to the students, "It is the hardest thing in the service—to do well." [1] On the other hand, if the minister knows how to read, he is likely to be in demand by the congregation which believes what the Book says about its own inspiration. Before we turn directly to the subject, however, let us think about the responsive reading.

THE QUESTION ABOUT THE RESPONSIVE READING

Opinions here differ sharply. Out of fifty bulletins from large, representative congregations from the Atlantic to the Pacific, approximately half show the use of the responsive reading on Sunday morning, and half do not. A generation ago the minister who wished to be up with the times was either using the responsive reading, or else

---

[1] *The Mystery of Preaching,* 1924, p. 235. This is one of our best books about preaching, with a good chapter about public worship.

wondering why he was not. But now he finds that in the Riverside Church or the Madison Avenue Presbyterian Church in New York, as in Shadyside or the First Presbyterian Church of Pittsburgh, there seems to be no such reading. If he inquires, he soon discovers that his brethren have decided opinions on the subject. Although the matter is not vital, it should be interesting.

Here is the gist of the argument, pro and con. The advocate of the responsive reading insists that it is biblical, and that there should be in the hour of worship a large use of the Scriptures; that the responsive reading affords every person an opportunity to take part in reading the Word of God, and that the exercise appeals especially to the boys and girls; that the reading calls for expression, not impression, and thus binds the people together, likewise preparing them for what is to come. The reply is that the Psalms were written to be sung, not to be read; that the responsive reading consumes valuable time, with no appreciable effect; and that it quickly becomes formal, almost perfunctory. The feeling is that if the minister reads well he ought to interpret each passage as a whole, and that if he does not read well he probably lacks a sense of rhythm, so that he cannot read well responsively. The chief argument, of course, is that in practice the reading is not effective.

Which plan is the better? Although the trend seems to be away from the practice, some of us still favor the use of the responsive reading. It should be possible for any thoughtful minister to avoid the faults common in such reading. One fault is in forgetting the purpose, which is to promote worship, not to teach a lesson; to express feeling, not to undergird the sermon. Hence the reading is closer akin to the music than to the preaching. Another frequent fault, due partly to the editors of our hymnals, is in the nature of the passage. James Black told the students in Richmond that he had enjoyed all the responsive readings he had heard in America, but that the passage was not always adapted to the purpose. The passage should be poetical, not prosaic; and from the Psalms, or other poetical parts of the Bible, not from the didactic parts of the Epistles. The passage should be comparatively short, and a lyrical unit, such as the ninety-first psalm. Occasionally it is feasible to have a concert reading, such as the Beatitudes, or the Ten Commandments.

If the responsive reading is to be effective, the minister must plan. When he announces the selection, if he makes any such announcement, he should give every person time to locate the passage. In phrasing the few introductory words, he may well remember the strangers: "In the psalter, in the back of the hymnal, let us read responsively selection number six." Then he should keep silent, letting the organist play a brief interlude. If he said, "selection six, page three hundred fifteen, psalm one hundred forty-five," there would be needless confusion. But why make such announcements, if there is a bulletin or a bulletin board? After the first week or two, if the minister introduces the new plan tactfully, the people will turn to the passage at the proper time. In any case they ought to rise, not only because they will read better, but because such a posture shows reverence for the Word of God.

In the actual reading, the minister's part is to lead. In the opening verse, he should set the pace, which should not be too fast, and he should keep this same tempo throughout. If he wishes to keep the people's responses from dragging, especially towards the end of the passage, he should take up each alternate verse as soon as they have finished the one preceding. Since the purpose of the reading is devotional, not didactic, he should follow the beat of the passage, and thus call little attention to the striking word or phrase. While the manner of reading here differs from that in the main lesson, in each case the effectiveness depends largely upon the skill of the minister. If anyone questions the popular effectiveness of the responsive reading, let him enjoy such an experience on a Sunday morning at Chautauqua under the leadership of President Arthur E. Bestor, or at Princeton under Charles R. Erdman.

When the people do their part of the reading well, there is usually a definite reason. Probably there is some one leading voice, or a number of leading voices, so that the people can follow with ease and assurance. In the Brown Memorial Church of Baltimore, a few years ago, the responsive reading and the congregational singing were so effective that the visiting minister asked for an explanation. It proved to be quite simple. In the quartet, the leading voice was that of the baritone; so the chairman of the music committee requested all four musicians to lead in the responsive reading, and to sing the hymns in unison. With such strong, expert, rhythmical leadership, the responsive reading was so inspiring that it led up naturally to the singing of the "Gloria."

Here, then, is another opportunity for the minister to train his people in the fine art of public worship. Instead of scolding them for not reading well, or urging them to do so, let him remember those three "Laws of Learning," [2] and then go to work. In the pastor's class, he can explain what he wishes to accomplish in this part of worship, and then read with the boys and girls the passage for next Sunday, thus showing them how they can help him every Sunday morning. Likewise can he present the matter at the midweek meeting, using much the same method. Ere long, the people's habits should be fixed aright, and then the bulletin may voice his appreciation: "The minister is grateful to the members of the choir and the congregation, especially the boys and girls, for the way in which they enter into the responsive reading."

THE READING OF THE MAIN LESSON

"The reading of the Scriptures ought always to be set in the centre of the service, where the light falls directly upon it. Compared to it, our own poor bits of sermons are a very trivial affair, a mere footnote in small print." [3]

[2] See page 122.
[3] *In Christ's Stead,* Warrack Lectures, Doran, 1925, p. 45.

These are the words of Arthur J. Gossip, of Glasgow. This brilliant preacher quotes John Wesley as saying that a certain congregation ought to pay its clergyman for not reading aloud from the Bible. Fortunately, however, any man whom God calls to lead in worship can learn how to read effectively from the Bible. Let him begin by thinking about the place of the Scriptures in the public worship of God.

In the Christian Church the minister is the man behind the Book. There is a beautiful symbolism in putting him behind the Book, and in keeping it open throughout the service. The pulpit Bible should be attractive and impressive in appearance, without gaudy ribbons to get tangled up by clumsy hands. It should be spotless and entire, as well as free from foreign matter. It should be fixed at the proper height, and it should lie open at the place of the morning lesson. It should always receive reverent, loving care. If the minister wishes to pound something solid, let him pound his own head. In public, as in private, let him beware against making any person laugh by twisting the words of the Holy Scriptures. As Phillips Brooks says, "Such jokes take the bloom off a young minister's life." [4]

The selection of the passage calls for loving care. Every lesson should be a complete unit. It may be a psalm, a parable, or a brief chapter, such as Paul's "hymn of Christian love." Usually, the passage is much too long. When one reads the parable of the Good Samaritan, why should

---

[4] *Yale Lectures on Preaching,* E. P. Dutton and Co., 1877, p. 55.

one read on about Mary and Martha?[5] When one reads the matchless poem about the Suffering Servant, however,[6] why should one not read all five strophes? Is there anything sacrosanct about these modern chapter and verse divisions, some of which are almost ludicrous? But when the chapter forms the natural unit, as in the twelfth of Romans, the obvious thing is to read it all. Even if the chapter is long, as in the twenty-seventh of the Acts, there ought to be time for such a thrilling narrative.

The best version for public reading is probably the King James. In spite of its well-known defects, such as the lack of division into paragraphs, and the presence of occasional infelicities, the King James Version is dear to the hearts of God's people. As the old lady says, "If it was good enough for the Apostle Paul it is good enough for me." What Scripture she knows is likely to be from this old version, which seems to be the best of all as a classic piece of English prose. As for the infelicities, one can usually avoid the most glaring, without calling attention to what one is doing. For example, in reading the familiar verse, "Whom do men say that I am?"[7] one simply says "Who," and goes on. In reading any one of the sixty-five verses where the King James says "cherubims,"[8] one merely says "cherubim," and thanks God for the treasure in this dear old earthen vessel. But still one will rejoice when the committee of scholars now at work under the International Council of Religious Education

---

[5] Luke 10:25-37, 38-42.   [6] Isa. 52:13—53:12.
[7] Matt. 16:13.   [8] E.g., Psalm 99:1.

brings forth the new translation, which is to remedy the defects of the King James, and still retain its wondrous charm.[9]

The preparation to read the passage calls for time and work. First of all, one should know exactly what it means, in its setting. Good reading is largely a matter of proper emphasis, and how can one interpret what one does not understand? After one sees what the passage means, one should read it aloud, more than once, preferably in the church and from the pulpit Bible. The reading should be deliberate, with significant pauses. But one should know where to pause, and how long. Like articulation, and everything else which enters into good reading, the mastery of the pause is usually the result of practice. So is the ability to make one's self clearly audible to the person who is slightly deaf, without seeming loud to the person whose hearing is acute. What a fine art is the worthy reading of the Scriptures![10]

The reading itself ought to be an act of worship. Hence one should announce the passage with care, as though one expected reverent attention to this message from the King Invisible. One should usually follow a set formula, naming the book, the chapter, and the verse, if that seems necessary. If one said, "the fifteenth chapter of First Corinthians, beginning at the thirty-fifth verse," who could remember all of that and quickly find the passage,

[9] See *The English Bible as Literature*, by Charles A. Dinsmore Houghton Mifflin Co., 1931.

[10] Cf. *Vocal and Literary Interpretation of the Bible*, by S. S. Curry, Hodder & Stoughton, 1912.

135

especially if one mouthed the words or mumbled them rapidly? After announcing the lesson, and the place where it is written, one waits until everything is still. Then one reads the passage, in accordance with its spirit, remembering that "emphasis is exposition."

The first law here is to honor the King, by making his message shine. The second is to remember one's hearer, so as to help him see the truth which will make him strong. The third is to call no attention to oneself. Really, all of this belongs under that first law, for in reading, as in everything else about public worship, the rule is—God first, the man in the pew second, and the leader third. So be sure to stand still. Make no gestures. Interject no comments. Only the occasional man, such as Spurgeon, can spend time profitably as a pulpit commentator. So let the Book speak for itself. Since it is impossible for the man in the pew to think about Christ and the reader at the same time, remember that saying of the Greeks, "Sir, we would see Jesus."

The man who reads well is tempted to call undue attention to the fact. James Denney used to say to many students of divinity at Glasgow, "Do not read those words as though you had written them yourself." According to a popular Presbyterian preacher and teacher, "Committing the Scriptures to memory, or almost so, is for most men an affectation, and is apt to get on the nerves of solicitous hearers, who dread the breakdown that some experience in such attempts. Also, it attracts undue attention to the speaker. Generally it is better to read from the accepted version of the congregation, and not from some palm-sized little book whose very appearance sacrifices dignity." [11] On a special occasion, however, such as the Lord's Supper, or a funeral, it is good to be able to speak the Word of God straight from the heart. In each case, one tries to do what will honor the Lord.

The reading of the Scriptures in worship should be an act of faith. If the minister takes it seriously, and prepares aright, the people will respond. An occasional sermon about the Bible in Christian experience should help them to exalt the Book. One need not argue about it, or defend it, as though it were in danger of being condemned to death. One need only interpret, illuminate, and enforce what it says about itself, notably in the words of Isaiah about the rain and the snow,[12] and in the words of the Risen Lord: "Blessed is he that readeth, and they that hear the words of this prophecy, and keep those things which are written therein." [13]

THE USE OF A LECTIONARY

The public reading of the Scriptures is more certain to be a means of grace throughout the year if the minister uses a lectionary. Such a list of suggested readings for the Christian Year is to be found in almost every book of worship issued by one of the churches. For a lectionary of a different sort, see the suggestive book by A. Boyd

[11] *Ministerial Practices,* Cleland B. McAfee, Harper's, 1928, p. 54.
[12] Isa. 55:10, 11.
[13] Rev. 1:3.

Scott, *Preaching Week by Week*,[14] or the Scottish *Book of Common Order*, edited by Millar Patrick.[51] Better still, each minister can make such a list of his own, a new one every year, perhaps during the mid-summer holiday. Here is a fascinating way to study the Bible. The lectionary at the close of this chapter represents how one man chooses such readings for the Christian Year.

The advantages of using a lectionary are varied. This plan ought to protect the people from hearing the same passages again and again, as well as enable them to hear the golden passages often. In almost every pulpit Bible, there are noteworthy passages, such as Isaiah forty, which seem never to have been read, and others, such as Isaiah fifty-three, which have been read repeatedly. The ideal is that of the United Church in Canada: "The Lord's people should hear the great passages at least once a year. So should they hear other passages, but only such as are suitable for public worship. If the minister has such a list before him, from week to week, and feels free to depart from it whenever he ought to read something else, he can save his time when time is precious, and still be sure that his selection will be a means of blessing.

The lectionary follows the Christian Year, but not in a wooden way. A lesson is something to be taught, and the successive lessons ought to follow some order, preferably that of time. Under any good plan there is both continuity and progress, from week to week, leading

---

[14] *The Warrack Lectures on Preaching,* Hodder & Stoughton, London, 1929, pp. 235-256.
[15] Oxford University Press, 1928.

up to the red-letter days of the Church. Thus in turn one presents every vital truth, and every impelling duty. The emphasis is chiefly upon the New Testament, particularly as one draws near to Easter. One way of planning is to take the New Testament lesson from the same Gospel every Sunday between Christmas and Easter. The idea is to ask the people to read from this one Gospel throughout the quarter. Many of them respond to such an invitation to do something specific, and find it increasingly profitable to read the Bible as it was written, a book at a time, ever keeping in view the central figure, Jesus Christ.

The wise use of a lectionary influences a man's preaching. While there is nothing about the plan which requires him to preach from any one passage, that is often exactly what he wishes to do. If the people are reading the Gospel of Luke—in this case, as in Matthew, the reading would begin about the middle of December—they will enjoy that reading all the more if they know that it will help them to appreciate the sermon next Sunday morning. Thus, in time, they should learn how to read the Bible for themselves, and how to use it as their guide-book in everyday living. They will think of their minister as the Interpreter, and thank God whenever they hear, or read, what John Bunyan wrote about such a man's portrait:

"It had eyes lifted up to heaven, the best of books in its hand, the law of truth was written upon its lips, the world was behind its back; it stood as if it pleaded with men, and a crown of gold did hang over its head."

Here is a suggested list of Bible readings for a year:

139

Looking Forward to Christmas

Isaiah 1:1-20	Romans 12:1-9
Isaiah 2:1-5	Romans 12:10-21
Isaiah 5:1-7	Romans 13:1-14
Isaiah 6:1-8	Romans 1:1-17
Isaiah 12:1-6	I Cor. 3:1-17
Isaiah 32:1-8	II Cor. 8:1-9
Isaiah 35:1-10	II Cor. 4:5-18
Isaiah 40:1-11, 28-31	Romans 8:1-17
Isaiah 52:13-53:12	Rev. 1:1-8
Isaiah 55:1-13	Rev. 22:1-7
Isaiah 61:1-11	Luke 1:26-38
Isaiah 62:1-12	Luke 1:39-56
Isaiah 9:2-7	Luke 2:8-20

Between Christmas and Easter

Luke 4:14-32	Romans 10:1-15
Luke 10:25-37	I Cor. 13:1-13
Luke 12:13-21	Romans 7:7-25
Luke 15:1-10	Romans 5:1-11
Luke 15:11-32	Romans 8:31-39
Luke 16:19-31	I Cor. 15:50-58
Luke 18:9-17	Eph. 6:10-20
Luke 19:1-10	II Cor. 5:1-10
Luke 23:1-26	II Cor. 5:11-21
Luke 23:27-38	Phil. 2:1-11
Luke 23:39-56	Romans 5:12-21
Luke 24:13-35	I Cor 15:1-28
Luke 24:36-53	I Cor. 15:35-49

The Afterglow of Easter

Acts 1:1-14	I Cor. 1:17-31
Acts 2:1-21	I Cor. 2:1-16
Acts 2:37-47	Eph. 2:1-10
Acts 5:1-11	Heb. 10:19-31
Acts 6:1-8	I Tim. 3:1-16
Acts 8:26-40	I John 1:1-10
Acts 9:1-9	II Cor. 3:1-18
Acts 9:10-22	James 5:7-20
Acts 12:1-19	Heb. 11:1-16
Acts 16:6-15	Heb. 11:32-40
Acts 16:25-40	Heb. 12:1-13
Acts 17:22-34	Heb. 12:14-29
Acts 18:1-11	I Pet. 2:11-25

Hope and Cheer for Summer Days

Psalm 8:1-9	Phil. 3:1-14
Psalm 19:1-14	II Tim. 3:14-17
Psalm 23:1-6	I Thess. 4:13-18
Psalm 24:1-10	II Pet. 1:1-11
Psalm 27:1-14	I Pet. 4:12-19
Psalm 32, or 51	I John 2:1-17
Psalms 42 and 43	Phil. 4:4-7
Psalm 65, or 85	Gal. 6:1-14
Psalm 91:1-16	II Cor. 12:1-10
Psalm 103:1-22	Phil. 4:8-20
Psalm 119:9-16	Col. 3:1-17
Psalm 121:1-8	Eph. 3:14-21
Psalm 122:1-9	Eph. 5:25-33

CHAPTER VIII

THE MEANING OF THE PUBLIC PRAYERS

*T*HE most sacred function of the Christian ministry is praying," said Henry Ward Beecher. "Never in the study, in the most absorbed moments, never in any company, where friends are sweetest and dearest, never in any circumstances in life, is there anything that is to me so touching as when I stand, in ordinary good health, before my great congregation to pray for them. Hundreds and thousands of times as I rose to pray and glanced at the congregation I could not keep back the tears. . . . There is no time when Jesus is so crowned with glory. . . . It seems as if God permitted me to lay my hand upon the very Tree of Life, and to shake down from it both leaves and fruit for the healing of my people." [1] Such an exalted estimate leads us to inquire concerning the meaning of public prayer.

THE MEANING OF PRAYER AS SACRIFICE

In the Christian Church, public prayer largely takes the place of sacrifice in the Hebrew Church. According to the Shorter Catechism, "Prayer is the offering up of our desires unto God." In Hebrew worship, there were

[1] *Yale Lectures on Preaching,* Second Series, J. B. Ford & Co., New York, 1874, p. 46.

five sorts of sacrifices: the burnt offering, the sin offering, the trespass offering, the peace offering, and the meal offering. So in Christian worship, there are various sorts of prayers. Just as each of those sacrifices had its own specific purpose, which was clear to the priest, if not to the people, so is every prayer in Christian worship the expression of specific desires on the part of those who pray. In prayer, as in sacrifice, the chief desire is to be right with God, and then to do his holy will.

The determining factor in Christian prayer is the character of God. Instead of talking about faith in prayer, we ought to stress faith in God. "He that cometh to God must believe that he is, and that he is a rewarder of them that diligently seek him." [2] God is real. He is present. He is ready to hear, and to bless. These are the tacit assumptions whenever people pray. We need no magic means to induce his presence, or to persuade him to hear. Rather do we need his Holy Spirit to make us conscious of his presence, and of his readiness to help us here and now. When we come to him as our Father, because he is the Father of our Lord and Saviour, we are in a mood to pray.

The character of God is the basis of our belief that he is always able to answer prayer. Sometimes we try to encourage the practice of public prayer because of its effect upon ourselves. Surely there is such a subjective effect, but it depends largely upon our belief in God's readiness to answer. Otherwise, few of us would keep

[2] Heb. 11:6.

143

on praying. Here is the testimony of perhaps the ablest living writer about the psychology of religious experience: "If the subjective value of prayer be all the value it has, we wise psychologists of religion had best keep the fact to ourselves; otherwise the game will soon be up, and we shall have no religion left to psychologize about." [3]

On the human side, the value of public prayer depends largely upon the attitude of the man in the pew. In the same place, and at the same time, one man may receive a blessing, and the next one may not. As the first man enters the sanctuary, his heart is filled with a sense of expectancy. During the prelude from the organ he is waiting quietly upon the Lord, in a spirit of receptivity. When the time comes for vocal prayer, especially the confession of sins, he is no longer passive and receptive; he responds to God's revelation of his glory, and joins with others as they pour out their souls in the expression of their desires. Here, then, is the ideal attitude in prayer: expectancy, receptivity, responsiveness—all in the spirit of fellowship. It should be evident that, apart from crying out for the pardon of sins, only the Christian can really pray.

The prayers of such a believer are the outpourings of his heart. Prayer is the expression of feeling, not of thought. In prayer as in preaching, both feeling and thought are present, but in prayer the feeling is more active and more prominent than in the preaching. In public prayer, the minister is voicing the feelings of those

[3] *The Religious Consciousness,* by James B. Pratt, Macmillan, 1928, p. 326.

in the pews, either what they feel, or what they should feel, as they are consciously in the presence of God. Here is the feeling of dependence upon him as the Creator and the Giver, the feeling of shame because we have not been worthy of such a holy God, the sense of relief because of his assurance that he has forgiven, the feeling of thankfulness for all his mercies, the desire for his blessing upon ourselves and upon every person or cause that is dear to our hearts, the desire to dedicate ourselves, one by one, to his service, for Jesus' sake. Yes, public prayer is the offering up of the desires of God's people.

THE MEANING OF THE DIFFERENT PRAYERS

In any one hour of worship, each prayer should have a meaning all its own. While every minister should plan in his own way, the order of the prayers usually follows the statement above, which calls for some sort of invocation, confession of sins, with assurance of pardon, thanksgiving, petition and supplication, and dedication by the worshiper. Whatever the order which any man follows, he should keep it in mind as he prepares to lead in worship every week, lest he fail to voice some of these ever-present desires of human hearts. So should he prepare to avoid overlapping and undue repetition of content. In other words, he should plan for each prayer in turn, according to its purpose.

First of all comes the invocation. This is often the most difficult prayer to plan, partly because it is largely

145

objective. The purpose is to express the desires of the people to become conscious of God's presence and to receive his blessing. As a rule, a man prepares an invocation of his own, being sure to make it short and simple. But he may use a historic prayer of the Church. For this purpose the collect serves admirably. Here is one which is deserving of study as a model: "Almighty God, unto whom all hearts are open, all desires known, and from whom no secrets are hid; cleanse the thoughts of our hearts by the inspiration of thy Holy Spirit, that we may perfectly love thee, and worthily magnify thy holy name, through Christ our Lord. Amen."

Every once in a while the minister may make a collect of his own and use it as the invocation. He will find that the collect is a complete sentence, in five distinct parts: first, the address, usually to the Father, sometimes to the Son, occasionally to the Holy Spirit; second, the relative clause, concerning some attribute of God, or else one of his promises; third, the petition, which is a simple statement of desire; fourth, the purpose in making this petition; fifth, the conclusion, which gives the ground for making the prayer. At the beginning of the hour, if spoken distinctly, deliberately, and with a sense of holy awe, the collect should catch and hold attention, as well as enlist the co-operation of the people. Such a prayer tends to give the entire hour a sense of dignity and elevation.[4]

[4] In *The Art of Public Worship,* by Percy Dearmer, Morehouse, 1919, see the chapter, "The Art of Making Collects."

After the invocation, there is a pause. Then the people confess their sins, perhaps by following in silence what the minister says in their stead, but preferably by repeating with him a form of sound words, such as that in the Protestant Episcopal *Book of Common Prayer*. If the hymnal does not contain one or two forms of confession, the officers may have two of them printed or mimeographed and pasted on the inside of the back cover. Like the invocation, this confession calls for deliberate utterance. Then there is a brief pause, after which the minister solemnly voices the assurance of God's pardon. Then follows a song of praise. Thus the opening prayer, with its three distinct parts, takes only a little time, less than one uses here in writing about it. The controlling purpose is to lead the people, one by one, into right relations with God, at the beginning of the service.

The next prayer is usually one of thanksgiving. In the ideal order, this prayer would include nothing else. In the Sunday morning service at the amphitheater in Chautauqua, after the anthem the people rise and join with the leader in saying those memorable words which one finds in almost every denominational book of worship: "Almighty God, Father of all mercies, we do give thee humble and hearty thanks." This entire prayer includes only one hundred thirty-one words. When spoken with due deliberation, it requires scarcely a minute. But in many a congregation which is not yet accustomed to the use of artistic forms, it would scarcely be wise to suggest the use of such a printed prayer, at least not

147

before they begin to love what seems to them "new ways of worship." In all such matters, the wise minister moves slowly, but still he moves.

Ideally, there should be one dominant element in each prayer. As a result, there would be an increased number of prayers in the hour, and each prayer would be shorter than it usually is in practice. In prayer, as in preaching, we are not heard for our much speaking. Psychologically, it is not wise to combine diverse elements in one omnibus effort, involving a strain on the attention of the man in the pew. Like the other parts of public worship, prayer should be restful, at least for the man who is a devout believer. But if, in deference to custom, it seems wise to combine the confession of sins with the invocation, and the words of thanksgiving with the other parts of the pastoral prayer, it should still be possible to make each prayer reasonably short. After all, a prayer is no longer than it seems.

The pastoral prayer is the most important of all, and likewise the longest. But still it should not be long. A well-known minister, who includes in it thanksgivings, petitions, and supplications, thinks of the pastoral prayer in terms of three minutes. Surely the upper limit should be less than five. When a man has prepared aright, he can say a vast deal in three minutes.

In the thanksgivings he may follow the general order of the one hundred third psalm, which begins with praises to God for his tender mercies to his children, one by one, and then leads out into the larger circles of life. Instead of striving to conjure up reasons for which no one else ever dreamed of being grateful, the minister seeks to express the gratitude of everyone present, and also to lead everyone in the expression of feelings which have been vainly struggling for utterance. Here at its best is Christian optimism.

The next element in pastoral prayer is usually petition. Between the words of thanksgiving and those of petition, there should be a pause, and then there should be a change of pitch, probably to a lower key. Here again, one is likely to begin with the individual and lead out into the larger circles of life and work represented in the congregation. In a somewhat different way from week to week, one is careful always to pray for the boy and the girl, the youth and the aged saint, as well as the man or woman in the middle years of life. With Joseph Parker, one should remember that "in every pew there is at least one broken heart." So the prayers for the sick, the lonely, and the sorrowing should somehow lead up to at least a glimpse of the life everlasting.

Then come the supplications. But between this new part of the prayer and the part preceding there should be another pause, with a change of tone. Technically, the distinction between petition and supplication is that in one the minister is expressing the desires of the people for themselves, whereas in the other he is voicing their desires for mankind. In practice, there is a distinct advantage in keeping the two parts separate. While no man with the shepherd heart would fail to present before

149

God the needs of his friends in the pews, and of those whom they love, there is a subtle temptation to neglect the prayers for our rulers, for world peace, and for the coming of the Kingdom throughout the world. After such intercessions, the people should be ready to unite in repeating the Lord's Prayer.

Somewhere in the heart of the service, there should be a little time for silent prayer. One good place is between the petitions and the intercessions. In the pastoral prayer no man is able to voice all the needs, the hopes, and the fears of the waiting people. Some of the older people may feel that they can do their silent praying at home, and that they pay the minister to pray in public. But gradually they will learn why the Friends love to wait silently upon the Lord, in the place where they meet to worship him. The young people who have come home from college are almost sure to enjoy the semi-mystical leadership of the man who encourages them to commune with God in the quietness of the sanctuary. Like every other act in public worship, silent prayer is largely a matter of habit, a habit which has long since justified itself in the experience of God's people.

Conscientious objectors are likely also to look askance at the "bidding prayer." But they should be mollified when they learn that it has had a long and honorable history in the various branches of the Church. In one of the various forms, the minister quietly explains what he is about to do, and then calls upon the people to thank God for particular reasons, or objects, one by one. After each of these calls he pauses, giving the person in the pew time to order his prayer aright. After naming a number of reasons for thanksgiving, the minister reads a collect. In like manner, he may use this way of leading the people in their prayers for themselves, and again in their prayers for others. If he uses the plan aright, and prepares as thoroughly as if he were to do all the speaking, he will find that the bidding prayer has unexpected possibilities.

Another way to secure wholesome variety and spiritual helpfulness is to use a litany. This form of prayer is even more ancient and honorable than the one described above. The litany seems to go back to the synagogue. It consists of a number of petitions, or supplications, in which the minister prays for a brief while, after which the people respond with a still shorter expression of their hearts' desires. In the liturgical churches, the litany is highly standardized. Elsewhere, it is usually simple, and it may assume any one of various forms. It lends itself admirably to the needs of a special occasion. In the Methodist Church, for example, the litany forms an important part of the beautiful "Order for the Administration of the Lord's Supper." Here at Princeton, former President J. Ross Stevenson often used at the Sacrament the sort of litany which is well known in the Church of Scotland.

Whatever its form, the pastoral prayer is an unintentional revelation of the minister's soul. Here comes to light the wealth or the poverty of his devotional life, the faithfulness or the lack of it in his pastoral labors, and the breadth or the narrowness of his unifying theology.

In a high sense, "Prayer time is God's punishment time." In another sense, pastoral prayer is a holy privilege, second to none on earth. It is much more likely to seem so if the minister forgets about himself and pours out before the Lord the desires of the waiting people. One of the noblest tributes to such a leader is that of a friend in speaking about the President of our Seminary: "He is a statesman in the Kingdom of God, but he never has lost his concern for the individual; and whenever he leads in public prayer, he expresses what I have long desired to say, but have never known how."

Not long after the pastoral prayer usually comes the one over the offering. In some churches the prayer comes before the offering, but some prefer to have it after. If it came before, it would express the desire of the people to dedicate themselves and their substance to God. When it comes after, the people may rise and sing the Doxology, which would be too exalted if it came at the beginning of the hour. In any case, the minister sets apart the gifts of the people by a brief prayer, somewhat as he does with the bread and wine in the celebration of the Sacrament. If the men who bear the gifts to the altar are those who give largely of their time and thought in handling the business of the church, he may well pray for them at times, and for God's blessing upon their labor of love.

This prayer is usually about as long as a collect. In fact, a collect often serves admirably. Again, one may use a verse of Scripture[5] as the substance for a prayer of

[5] E.g., Acts 20:35; II Cor. 8:9; Mal. 3:10.

his own phrasing. Here is one which is homemade: "O Lord our God, in thy great lovingkindness thou hast opened the windows of heaven and poured out upon us blessings so rich and vast that there is not room in our hearts and lives to receive them all. Of thine own we bring a portion unto thee. We beseech thee to cleanse our gifts and to use them for thy glory, through Jesus Christ our Lord. Amen" Instead of striving to phrase a new prayer of this sort every week, the minister can use the same forms again and again, at intervals, so that the people will come to know a few of these prayers by heart.

The prayer after the sermon is equally short, and much more vital. Unlike the prayer over the offering, this one is individual, not collective. It voices the one prevailing desire in the heart of the person in the pew. In the message, the aim has been to lead this person to resolve with Isaiah, "Here am I; send me." So the prayer should express this new determination to dedicate life and service to God in the particular way which he has made clear and luminous in the sermon. Like the closing part of the sermon, this prayer calls for careful planning, lest it say too little or too much. It is so short and so simple that it should linger in the heart of the worshiper as he goes to his home.

Last of all is the benediction. It deserves vastly more attention than it usually receives, for it is no mere polite way of putting the period at the end of the hour. The benediction is an act of God, in which he bestows his grace upon those who are ready to receive it by faith.

153

Since this is the crowning moment in life's holiest hour, the minister should set the example of high regard for the benediction. One way to do so is to make a list of those in the Bible, and especially the three which are most common in the Church.[6] Here is another which has won favor: "The peace of God, which passeth all understanding, keep your hearts and minds in the knowledge and love of God, and of his Son Jesus Christ our Lord; and the blessing of God Almighty, the Father, the Son, and the Holy Ghost, be amongst you, and remain with you always. Amen." One of these four is almost certain to fit the tone color of any service.

Whatever the benediction, the minister should repeat it exactly, word for word. Any attempt to "improve" it would be an impertinence. The only thing to do with such holy words is to let them find their way into the hearts and lives of God's people. Even a little carelessness on the part of the leader may detract from the force of the inspired words. In the Apostolic Benediction every Sunday why should one begin with "Now may," thus transforming this wondrous means of grace into an uncertain petition? In the Covenant Benediction from the Epistle to the Hebrews, though one begins with "Now," why should one close by saying, "now and forevermore"? Surely the exact words of the Bible are best. Fortunately one seldom alters the wording of the Priestly Benediction, although one may use it with those blessed words from

[6] II Cor. 13:14; Heb. 13:20, 21; Num. 6:24-26.

Paul about "the peace of God which passeth all understanding." [7]

Any real benediction calls for memorable utterance. While the people bow down as a symbol of their readiness to receive God's manifold grace, or else stand with bowed heads, the minister's hands are uplifted as a symbol of God's blessing. The rate of speech is deliberate, and there is a pause after each important phrase. "The grace of the Lord Jesus Christ —and the love of God—and the communion of the Holy Ghost—be with you all. Amen." Then let there be silence in the church.

Glancing back, we note that each prayer has its own special purpose. While the benediction is more than a prayer, for convenience we are putting it with these other acts of worship. Since the spiritual value of these prayers depends a good deal upon the participation of the man in the pew, would it not be well to explain to him the meaning of public prayer in general, and of these prayers which enter largely into every hour of public worship? If the minister is the home missionary of music, and if he guides the people in hearing the Scriptures, should he not also instruct them concerning the holy privilege of corporate prayer?

THE MEANING TO THE LAYMAN

In many congregations the prayers mean little or nothing to most of the people. As one man said about his idea of God, the impression made by our prayers is

[7] Phil. 4:7.

something of "an oblong blur." The people may not mean to be critical; they are more likely to be confused. For example, if on a Monday morning the minister asks two or three of his most thoughtful laymen, each by himself, to state the purpose or the general content of each prayer in the morning service the day before, the replies are likely to be disheartening. Through no fault of their own, the laymen are often as ignorant about such things as seminary students used to be in the good old days when the curriculum gave no place to public worship. How, then, can one show these lay friends the meaning of the prayers?

One way is through the bulletin. Before me lies the printed order of service in use at Trinity Presbyterian Church, Birkenhead, England. With each prayer is a clear statement of its purpose. Of the twenty-nine lines showing the order on Sunday morning, fourteen have to do directly with the prayers. The order itself, in red and black, is a model of the printer's art. Not only does such a statement help the visiting minister to order his prayers aright; it should help the people actually to pray. In the bulletin one can also have an occasional word about prayer; it may be an apt quotation from one of the books named at the end of the present volume. Sometimes there is the text of a prayer, by the minister, or from one of the books—a prayer which he wishes the people to say with him in the service. Why not use the bulletin for the things which matter most?

A more direct way is to preach about public prayer.

156

Every minister preaches often about prayer,[8] but probably not often enough about it in public worship. For example, here is a sermon about prayer as sacrifice.[9] The basic truth is the priesthood of believers. Somehow the minister makes it clear that while he is the leader in public prayer, all of God's people together are offering sacrifices acceptable to God. Unlike people who sit on the side lines and watch some athlete show his dexterity, those who worship God in spirit and in truth enter actively into every part of public worship, especially the prayers.

Another way to promote intelligent prayer in church is to use the Junior Sermon. The time allotted is just about long enough to permit one to make clear and luminous the meaning of the invocation, or of the prayer over the offering. The man who knows how to talk to boys and girls in church will be able to make such a message glow. The result will be a lifelong impression upon the heart of many a boy who will some day be an officer in the church, if not a minister. Many a girl will later be all the more ready for marriage and motherhood because she has learned the meaning of prayer. As a by-product of such teaching, many an adult will begin to take a more intelligent part in the prayers. And so the minister will have all the more reason to prepare for this part of his leadership.

There is need, also, for an occasional sermon about one

---

[8] Cf. *Lord, Teach Us to Pray*, Sermons by Alexander Whyte, Doran.
[9] I Pet. 2:5*b*.

of the benedictions. Where could one find a more fruit-ful text than any of those major benedictions, and a more fruitful subject than the Trinity? This is the direct teach-ing of the Apostolic Benediction, and the indirect teach-ing, in words of rare beauty, of the Priestly Benediction. As for the Covenant Benediction, though the message here is not easy to present, it is glorious. After any of these sermons the hearer should have a new reason for joy in God, and he should henceforth look upon the bene-diction as one of the most blessed means of grace.

The best way of all to guide the people into learning how to pray in public is to pray for them in private. Often throughout the week, and above all on Saturday evening, after everything for the morrow is ready, it is good to commit the service to God, as an act of faith, and then go through the roll of the members, praying for them one by one. In praying for a certain young man, one may use the words of the prophet, "Lord, I pray Thee, open his eyes, that he may see." [10] After all, it is only God who can teach his people to pray.

[10] II Kings 6:17.

CHAPTER IX

THE FINE ART OF LEADING IN PRAYER

MANY a minister longs to be able to lead in prayer more effectively Such a man is likely to underestimate his ability, but surely there is room for everyone to improve. The difficulty is that no one of us is worthy to teach anyone else. Practically all that one can do is to set up certain ideals about this fine art of leading in prayer, point out some of the most frequent faults, of which a man is likely to be unconscious, and then suggest certain practical ways of carrying out these ideals so as to be reasonably free from these faults. Such is the trail before us now.[1]

THE IDEAL OF PUBLIC PRAYER

The quality of a man's prayers in public depends largely upon his ideals of prayer. These, in turn, come to him in various ways, notably through the study of the subject in the Bible. The section at the end of this chapter suggests a way of mastering the public prayers of the Bible, one by one. Any man who follows such a course of quiet study at home will find that his ideals about this fine art will keep rising from month to month;

[1] Cf. *Reality in Worship*, by Willard L. Sperry, Macmillan, 1926, pp. 304-332.

and though he may not be conscious of the fact, his attainments will also keep rising. If the discussion which follows is more about form than substance, the reason is because we are thinking about worship as a fine art.

First, every prayer in public worship should have a pattern all its own. The pattern depends upon the purpose. As a rule, each prayer should have much the same pattern from week to week, so as to make it easier for the person in the pew to pray. In the pastoral prayer, especially, the pattern should stand out. In the Lord's Prayer, which is our model, there is a simple twofold structure, according to which we pray for the coming of the Kingdom and then for the supply of our personal needs. In the High Priest's Prayer[2] there is a threefold climactic framework, leading up to petitions for "the holy Church throughout the world," as we sing in the "Te Deum." As in a sermon, the structure of a prayer calls for unity, so that there is only one prayer, with its different parts; order, so that each part comes in due succession; symmetry, so that each part receives the attention which its importance deserves, but no more; and progress, so that there is cumulative feeling as one draws towards the close. This is what one of our most helpful books means by "The Architecture of Prayer." [3]

Second, so should every prayer have a style all its own. In general, the style of public prayer is notable for simplicity and clearness, as well as for human interest and

[2] John 17.
[3] *Extempore Prayer*, by M. P. Talling, Manchester, 1902, chap. viii.

quiet beauty. The clearness is due to the fact that the leader knows whither he is going and how he plans to get there, and likewise to the fact that he is voicing feelings rather than thoughts. The simplicity is due to the fact that he thinks of himself as a sort of elder brother talking with the Father God on behalf of other members of one large family, and that he has no reason for self-display. The element of interest is more difficult to analyze. The secret is in expressing the feelings of one's friends. As for beauty, that is almost beyond the reach of our words.

For an example of such a prayer, turn to the longest one in the Bible, the one by Solomon at the dedication of the Temple.[4] Here is unity in the midst of variety, order in which every paragraph stands out by itself, progress towards a worthy end, and symmetry like that of a copper beech or a hemlock tree. Here, too, is the sort of rhythmical prose which one finds at its best in certain parts of the Bible. Here are sentences balanced according to the artistry of Hebrew parallelism, and yet there is a forward movement like that of a river on its way to the sea. Best of all is the refrain, which sounds forth eight times, "Hear thou in heaven thy dwelling place, and when thou hearest, forgive."

The style of a public prayer differs from the style of a sermon much as the literature of feeling differs from that of thought. In prayer, as in preaching, both feeling and thought should be present; but in prayer the feeling

[4] I Kings 8:12-61.

should prevail. While many a sermon should be more beautiful than it is—in order to make known the truth about "Fairest Lord Jesus, Ruler of all nature"—a man's prayers should be still more deeply interfused with the beauty of holiness. This sort of beauty, however, comes best when a man's heart is intent upon something higher. If he loves God, and if he sympathizes with the people, whom he loves for the Master's sake, he can trust his heart to clothe each of his prayers in a garment of beautiful words. According to psychology, when a man's heart is moved, his words tend to flow in a pleasing rhythm.

The beauty of a prayer depends largely upon the sentences and the words. While the tendency in modern preaching is towards the short, crisp sentence, there is still a place in prayer for the longer sentence, especially if it keeps moving forward. While a good many people admire sparkling phrases and striking epigrams, which raise a certain kind of sermon above mediocrity, there is no place for that sort of thing in public prayer. It is a safe rule to use no sentence, phrase, or word that will call attention to itself. The reason is because no one in church can think about the minister and God at the same time. Hence one should confine oneself almost wholly to the sort of words which abound in the King James Bible, and in *Pilgrim's Progress*. The man who keeps his soul saturated in the Bible, and in Bunyan, will learn to pray with words of quiet beauty.

Third, these same principles apply to delivery, a word

which one hesitates to use concerning public prayer. Here, too, the need is for simplicity and clearness, human interest and quiet beauty. Here, too, there is nothing which calls attention to oneself. When a man leads in public prayer, the best voice is the one that never is heard. While clearly audible, even to the person who is somewhat dull of hearing, the leader's voice keeps to the lower ranges, and so is pleasing to the more sensitive ear. Every once in a while, a person hears such a speaking voice over the radio. That is an opportunity to study the secret of effective utterance in prayer. Meanwhile, here is the ideal: "The Lord God hath given me the tongue of the learned, that I should know how to speak." [5]

Fourth, and most vital of all, the spirit of prayer should be worshipful. When the man at the altar is really praying, the spirit of what he is doing becomes contagious. On the human side, the secret is sympathy. Here is the elder brother pleading with the Father God on behalf of his needy children, whether they are sinners or saints. Such a spirit of sympathy breathes through every word from Judah when he pleads with the Governor of Egypt for the life of innocent Benjamin. [6] This is one of the most moving passages in the Old Testament. In secular literature, think of *The Heart of Midlothian,* one of Scott's novels which should mean much to the minister. Here is Jeanie Deans, pleading with Queen Caroline for the life of sinning sister Effie. When the life of a dear one is at stake, a person finds words to ex-

[6] Gen. 44:18-34. [5] Isa. 50:4.

press his feelings. In order to pray aright, therefore, one needs to feel aright towards God, and towards those for whom one prays.

THE WEAKNESSES OF PUBLIC PRAYER

In bald American prose, the most common faults in public prayer seem to be six.[7] First, many a prayer lacks the note of reality. This part of a minister's duties tends to become mechanical. One reason is because he has to pray often, and sometimes without preparation. On a given Lord's Day, including family devotions, the minister may try to lead some of the same people to the throne of God fifteen or twenty times. He may spend more minutes in these public, or semi-public, prayers than he has spent in private devotions throughout the preceding week. If so, is it any wonder that he often seems to be "all prayed out," and that his "long prayer" seems like Lincoln's steamboat, with its six-foot boiler and its ten-foot whistle? Yet he may wonder why his young people are growing restive, and why the large congregation in quest of a pastor turns to the young man who is being graduated from the seminary. With all of his imperfections on his head, the young minister would scarcely dare to enter the sanctuary to pray for others without first praying for himself.

Second, there is often a lack of proper purpose. Especially in the long prayer, while ostensibly addressing God, one may be actually trying to preach or teach; one may

[7] Cf. *Extempore Prayer,* by M. P. Talling, chap. ix.

be exhorting or scolding, flattering some person, or else displaying one's powers. At daily chapel in Princeton College, former President McCosh once forgot to announce the change in the hour for a class in German, and so he embodied the news in his closing prayer. If any minister feels that he personally is free from this tendency to use the time of prayer to get something into the minds of the people, let him engage a stenographer to take down the words of his pastoral prayer, and then let him invite a lawyer, or a newspaper man, to delete everything which does not move Godward. What remains is likely to be a thing of shreds and patches.

Third, there is likely to be a lack of proper subject matter. In any one hour of worship the different prayers are usually too much like each other, and in any one of them from week to week there is a pitiful sameness. In the pastoral prayer, there may be only vague generalities, or else parochial commonplaces. At a time when the Church in many a land seems in danger of being snuffed out, it is possible to attend divine worship for six months without ever hearing a prayer for the lands across the sea. There may not even be a prayer for our own rulers. Even if they seem to belong to the wrong political party, they surely need the prayers of God's people. Still more strange is the absence of confession. Even in the holy minutes leading up to the Sacrament, the people may not come face to face with their sins. Fortunately, however, all these failings do not often appear in the same prayer.

Fourth, there is often weakness of structure. In fact,

there sometimes seems to be nothing of the sort. Perhaps this is partly why many a prayer lasting only five minutes seems interminable. Instead of leading through a land of hills and valleys, the minister seems to be wandering round in a wilderness, with nothing for the mind's eye to see, nothing for the heart to feel, nothing for the will to do. The fault, of course, is in the absence of a plan, and doubtless back of that is the lack of preparation. The ability to keep on talking without moving forward is even more deadening when a man prays in public than when he preaches. In either case, the remedy calls for fixing a purpose, and for work in the study. Meanwhile, such a minister may wonder why some of his people love to steal away to a church where the man of God knows how to pray.

Fifth, there is sometimes an unfortunate style. According to John Henry Jowett, the most popular evangelical preacher of yesterday, "We frequently fix upon the sermon when we seek to account for the comparative impotency of a service, when perhaps the real cause of paralysis is to be found in our dead and deadening prayers. There is nothing mightier than the utterance of spontanoeus prayer, when it is born in the depths of the soul. But there is nothing more dreadfully unimpressive than extemporary prayer which leaps about on the surface of things, a disorderly dance of empty words, going we know not whither, a mob of words carrying no blood, bearing no secret of the soul, a whirl of insignificant expressions, behind which is no vital pulse, no silent cry from lone and desolate depths." [8]

In such a substitute for a prayer, there is often undue familiarity in the use of our Lord's titles, with much meaningless repetition. Surely it is sufficient to say "O Lord," or "Heavenly Father," at the beginning of each new stage in the prayer. In fact, there may be such an address at the beginning of each paragraph. The difficulty is that there may be no paragraphs, so that the prayer flows along like a brook. In prayer, as in preaching, the minister who ignores the paragraph makes it hard for the layman to follow. Often, too, one is careless in the use of words which are slovenly, or even incorrect. One might almost as well appear in the pulpit wearing bedroom slippers. There may even be grammatical errors, such as "Forgive us of our debts," "We pray down thy blessing," and the improper use of "might." What is the matter with our American education?

The strange fact is that many a high school boy knows enough to sneer at his minister's literary style, especially in prayer. The student may indulge freely in slang, but he expects his minister to speak as correctly as the local teacher of English. So does the boy's father sometimes ask why the radio preacher never is guilty of a grammatical blunder, whereas the local minister makes a number in almost every prayer. When one of the best-known congregations in America was without a pastor, the committee investigated many a man near and far,

[8] *The Preacher, His Life and Work,* Hodder & Stoughton, 1912, p. 152.

only to report that with certain exceptions the clergymen in our country seem to be illiterate. Those laymen found that only an occasional minister seemed to be able to go through the hour of worship without making errors of which any high school student should be ashamed.

Sixth, there are often obvious faults in delivery. Here are words mispronounced, so that one says "wurshup," "Lead us snot," and "Lettuce spray." Often there is undue rapidity, and lack of sustained volume, so that the elderly person cannot hear the latter part of many a sentence. On the other hand, there may be too much sound and fury, signifying nothing. Fortunately, these faults yield to careful treatment. The difficulty is that as one grows older one is not conscious of these habits. Just as it is necessary to have one's automobile checked every six months by an expert, would it not be well for the minister once in a while to seek disinterested advice about his ways of public speech, especially in prayer?

THE PREPARATION OF THE PRAYERS

Any man who is called of God can learn to lead in prayer acceptably. How? Largely by preparing every week. In a sense, the prepared minister is better by far than his prepared prayers. When the man of spirituality and culture has to lead in public worship without adequate opportunity to prepare, he can pray well. But the strange fact is that this sort of man is the most likely to prepare when he can do so. One reason why many of us are hoping for a renaissance of public worship is because

168

the number of such men seems to be increasing. In general, they prepare in three different ways.

First, what seems the easiest way is openly to borrow and use a prayer of the Church. For the invocation, the prayer over the offering, or in the occasional "bidding prayer," a man may feel that a well-known collect from Chrysostom best fits the immediate need. Without apology, one commits the prayer to memory and recites it word for word, or else openly reads it from the notebook which contains everything one is to need during the hour of worship. The difficulty sometimes is to lay one's hand upon exactly the prayer which one desires. But, fortunately, as in searching for the right hymn or Scripture lesson, one is learning to know and to love the best sort of source book. In a few years one should secure and know intimately a number of the books, such as those suggested at the end of this volume.

Second, a more difficult way is to write out such a prayer of one's own, and speak it from memory or read it from the book. Another plan is to write it out and then use the substance. It is good to form the habit of writing out prayers, one a day, year after year, and then to store away at least the best. As in the art of playing the piano, mastery depends in large measure upon keeping in practice, provided one always practices with care. The prayer which a man writes may not sound much like one from *The Book of Common Worship,* but in prayer, as in preaching, what a man does himself is more likely to prove helpful to his people than what he borrows from a

169

spiritual genius. As in mastering any other art, sooner or later one finds oneself, and then the writing out of one's prayers from day to day becomes a source of joy.

Third, the most difficult plan is that of preparing only in outline and then letting the words come as they will. This is perhaps the most common way of getting ready for the pastoral prayer. In keeping with Alexander Maclaren's habit of committing to memory a sentence or two at the beginning of the sermon, as well as at the close, and then speaking ex tempore, one prepares the substance but not the form. If one is master of the spoken word, this way of leading in the pastoral prayer is admirable. But one must be willing to forgo the advantages of stately diction and faultless style. In childlike simplicity, one aims rather to express the desires of the friends in the pews, and to present the needs of the world which they ought to love. Needless to say, such a prayer sounds better to these friends who follow it because it voices the feelings of their hearts than to the visiting critic, who judges it as a piece of English prose.

In all these matters, each man ought to seek and follow the guidance of the Holy Spirit. Then each one will prepare in his own way. The resulting excellence is perhaps the rarest, as well as the finest, of ministerial accomplishments. In five years, or perhaps ten, any minister can fairly well master this finest of fine arts. But he will never rest content, for even the worthiest of human prayers is only an earthen vessel. The light must come from God. That, too, is in answer to prayer. "Lord, teach us to pray." [9]

THE PUBLIC PRAYERS OF THE BIBLE

From home study, one makes a fairly complete list, or else borrows from the book by J. E. McFadyen.[10] Then one concentrates upon a single prayer at a time, following a definite plan:

First, the external facts. Note the place, the occasion, the time of day, and the posture, with anything else that is significant.

Second, the subject matter. Is the prayer chiefly objective or subjective, individual or social, comprehensive or selective? Of the following, which predominates: adoration, confession, thanksgiving, petition, supplication, dedication? Of these moods, which prevails: a sense of expectancy, a feeling of God's presence, a consciousness of personal need, or a desire to be useful to men? Is the prayer suitable for divine worship today? If so, when and how?

Third, the literary form. Is the prayer notable for unity and order, symmetry and progress? Is the movement from the particular to the general, or the reverse? In the King James Version, is the style notable for beauty? Is there a quiet prose rhythm? Is the style figurative? Are the sentences long or short, simple or complex, balanced or not, memorable or commonplace? Are the

---

[9] Cf. *Self-Training in Meditation*, 1926, and *Self-Training in Prayer*, 1926, both by A. H. McNeile, D. Appleton Co.

[10] *The Prayers of the Bible.*

words Anglo-Saxon or Latin, popular or scholastic? Does the prayer belong to the literature of feeling, of thought, or of power?

Such a course leads up to a study in the prayers of our Lord. He who in the days of his flesh taught the disciples to pray is even more concerned about teaching a minister to pray than to preach.

CHAPTER X

THE PLAN OF THE ENTIRE SERVICE

THE time has come for us to think about the service as a whole. While it consists of hymns and prayers, readings from the Scriptures, and the sermon, the service as a whole is much more than the sum of the various parts. In fact, the content of the various parts ought to depend largely upon the purpose of the hour as a whole. Such a way of planning for the entire service, and for the various parts, calls for the use of the imagination, which is the synthesizing power. The minister who has this power and uses it aright in planning for public worship is an artist. Thus from week to week he is able to secure unity and variety, beauty and restfulness, as well as inspiration for the man in the pew to attempt the impossible, and to do it by the grace of God.

In the hour of worship there are likely to be three movements. According to Henry N. Wieman of the University of Chicago,[1] in the early part of public worship one should plan for "exposure"; in the next part, for "diagnosis"; in the latter part, for "adjustment." In each case the reference is to God and his holy will. Since the word "adjustment" sounds almost mechanical, perhaps

---

[1] *Methods of Private Religious Living*, Macmillan, 1929, p. 110.

one should say "acceptance." Even that does not suffi-
ciently make clear the carrying out of what the Great
Physician prescribes for the soul. From another point of
view, biblical rather than philosophical, the hour of worship ought to afford the layman a sort of mountain-top
experience, with three successive stages: the new revelation of divine glory, the new understanding of his own
life as it is in the eyes of God, and the new inspiration
for service.

In any such plan, the sermon is likely to gather up the
three movements and thus constitute a fourth. As Karl
Barth and Emil Brunner keep insisting, the sermon is a
present-day revelation of God's holy will, leading to the
searching of the hearer's soul, and then to the acceptance
of the newly revealed truth as it bears on his life among
men. Thus the sermon is an act of worship, an act
which means that the light of God is shining out today
through the pulpit.[2] If in this book there is little about
the sermon, one reason is because we sons of the Reformation are already aware of its high place in public worship.
Just now, in many quarters, the need is for emphasis
upon what we used to call "the setting of the sermon."
If in music and in prayer, as in reading from the Book,
the minister plans aright, the sermon will be doubly effective. On the Lord's Day there will be in his House
many a radiant face, and throughout the week there will

[2] Cf. *The Christian Preacher*, by Alfred E. Garvie, Scribner's, 1921, pp.
316-324.

be in the parish many a singing heart. How, then, shall one plan for such a service?

Every man should do this work in his own way. The pattern will depend largely upon his practical philosophy of preaching and worship. In other words, how can he exalt the sermon and still keep it in its place? Here are three ways which have commended themselves to men in the active ministry. Each way has advantages all its own.

First, the obvious way is that of the closely unified service. Here one prepares the sermon and then lets it dominate everything, with the possible exception of the pastoral prayer. Such a pathway is easy to mark out and follow. After a few years of practice, the minister who is familiar with his Bible and his hymnbook can lie down on the couch and mentally plan for the morning service in five or ten minutes. Sometimes the visiting minister at our seminary used to astound the students by seeming to prepare his order of service on Sunday morning, while the organist was playing the prelude. As a rule, this sort of extemporaneous leadership is worth little more than it costs. But, fortunately, it is possible to plan for the closely unified service with loving attention to every detail. The ideal here is that of King David: "Neither will I offer burnt offerings unto the Lord my God of that which doth cost me nothing." [3]

[3] II Sam. 24:24.

175

Here is the way the plan sometimes works. Since the sermon is to be about "The Christian Secret of Content-ment," one asks the organist for a soft, meditative pre-lude, of the sort that one wishes she would play more often; and for a "sweet and low anthem," which may be based upon Matthew 11:28-30. One chooses such hymns as "Spirit of God, descend upon my heart," "Im-mortal Love, forever full" ("We may not climb the heav-enly steeps"), and "Peace, perfect peace." The responsive reading is the ninety-first psalm, and the main lesson is Matthew 6:19-34, or else a part of Philippians 4. The prayers have to do with glad acceptance of God's holy will. The benediction is about the peace of God, and then the choir may softly chant the words of Charlotte Elliott, words which brought peace to the heart of Doctor Wilfred Grenfell on Easter Day, 1908, as he drifted out to sea on an ice-floe. Last winter these words formed the theme song of the Catholic Hour over the radio:

> "My God, my Father, while I stray
> Far from my home, on life's rough way,
> O teach me from my heart to say,
> 'Thy will be done!'"

After such an hour Sunday morning, one seeks for something decidedly different at night. So one may plan a sort of semi-military program. The sermon may be about "The Will of God in a World at War." The idea of loyalty to God in view of war may govern the choice of the hymns: "God of our fathers, whose almighty hand," "O God of love, O King of peace, make wars throughout the world to cease," and "Lord God of hosts, be with us yet, lest we forget, lest we forget." The Scripture lesson may be Micah 4:1-5, or else Romans 13:1-14; and the prayers may express the idealism of a Christian patriot. Such a service would have brought delight to the heart of former President Theodore Roosevelt, who rightly contended that many a sickly saint needs a blood transfusion of loyalty to both God and state.

This way of planning appeals to many a strong, thoughtful man of God. In his Yale Lectures, John Kelman says: "The structure of a single service shall be dominated by one subject throughout all its parts. . . . The bane of all our work is the distracted and discursive thinking upon religious things, which is the habit of very many of those to whom we preach." [4] In the hands of such a master as John Kelman, who used to enthrall the university students that came to hear him in Free St. George's, Edinburgh, the closely unified service makes a strong, lasting impression. As a rule, this way of planning appeals to the minister who is more intent upon influencing people than upon glorifying God. The purpose is likely to be didactic, rather than devotional.

The closely unified service lends itself admirably to the needs of a special occasion, such as Christmas or Easter, the dedication of the sanctuary, or the celebration of some anniversary. The occasion itself suggests various points of view, such as the past, the present, and the

[4] *The War and Preaching*, Yale University Press, 1919, pp. 164, 165.

future, so that it is easy to keep the worship moving forward, perhaps with cumulative effectiveness. The resulting impression should be wholesome and lasting. It is more likely to be so if the minister follows some other plan when there is nothing special. One of the surest ways of attracting favorable attention to one's special services is to make the worship on every such occasion different from that on other days.

As a rule, the morning hour should afford wholesome variety. When the worshiper enters the Lord's House and glances at the bulletin board, he should rarely be able to tell his wife the substance of the parson's sermon. The value of the message, as of other parts in public worship, depends somewhat upon the layman's feeling of expectancy. When the minister begins, no one should be able to tell in detail what he is about to do; and after he has finished, the thoughtful worshiper should be able to tell much that he has heard. In planning the regular meals for a hungry husband and hungry children, the wise mother does not think of having for breakfast nothing but sweet things; for lunch nothing but sour viands, and for dinner nothing but starchy food. Even if such fare were pleasing, it would not meet the needs of the body. So does the soul need a varied diet.

In the hour of worship there should be something to satisfy the heart hunger of every person present. In a spirit of wistful expectation, a godly woman from South Carolina went one night to a well-known church in New York City. For six weeks during the darkest part of

178

1917 she had been watching over her brother, who had contracted typhoid fever in one of the northern cantonments. When at last she dared to leave him, she went to church, hoping to find peace for her troubled heart. But the one thing on the preacher's mind that evening was Christian patriotism, with which her soul had long been aflame. Even in the prayers there was nothing to comfort the person who was suffering from the backwash of the war. After more than an hour, in which the prayers seemed to her to be only sermonettes, she stole out of the church and stumbled down the steps, scarcely able to see because of her blinding tears. Which of these two had the correct idea of public worship, the woman in the pew, or the man at the altar?

Second, a more difficult way to plan is that of the widely varied service.[5] The idea is to give expression to every worthy mood of the people, in the degree of its importance. As in the *Fifth Symphony* of Beethoven, or the *Communion Service* of the Protestant Episcopal Church, the various parts should blend in one united whole. Instead of beginning with songs, readings, and prayers about the Sacrament, that historic service begins with the people where they are, in the valley, and then gradually leads up to the mountain top. For example, as a reminder that they have sinned against God's holy law times without number, they join in repeating the Ten Commandments. In the non-liturgical churches, also,

---

[5] Cf. *The Mystery of Preaching,* by James Black, Revell, 1924, pp. 228-230.

179

the widely varied service may be admirable. But on the part of the leader it requires unusual ability, as well as the willingness to work.

Third, the most difficult and delicate way to plan is probably that of the alternating service. The idea is to keep the attention of the man in the pew shifting from the divine to the human, and then back to the divine. Instead of a single idea, which would dominate, or many ideas, which would harmonize, there are two ideas, which stand out in contrast. Such is the movement of thought and feeling in the account of Jacob's vision at Bethel. There the angels of God kept ascending and descending. The record does not seem to mean that there was one ascent and one descent, but that the going and the coming were more or less continuous. So in the hour of worship, the praises and the prayers of God's people keep ascending to him, and his mercies keep streaming down into the souls of his children.

There is such a twofold emphasis in Raphael's masterpiece, *The Transfiguration*. At first glance, there seems to be a lack of unity. On the mount one beholds the glory of the transfigured Christ, and at the foot one sees the plight of the demoniac lad. Actually the two parts of the picture are one, for the eyes of the lad are fixed upon the Lord, as he is high and lifted up in his transfigured glory. That scene on the mount is perhaps our noblest object lesson of what needy mortals should experience in the hour of worship. Now as then, there ought to be both the divine revelation and the human response. Everything centers in the Lord Jesus as he makes himself known through human beings. Little by little, those human faces should fade from view, until the man who worships should see no one but the Lord Jesus, and thus be transformed into his likeness.[6]

Here, then, are three ways of planning the hour of worship, and of course there are other ways. Let us think about these three ways of planning a service when one is preaching about the Holy Spirit, "The Power of God in the Lives of Men." Under the closely unified plan, every part of the service would have to do with the Holy Spirit, especially with what the fathers called his office work. In the widely varied service, some of these truths would gradually emerge in the course of worship that expressed many desires of the waiting hearts. According to the alternating plan, the attention of the person in the pew would keep shifting from the power and the glory of the Spirit to the weakness and the needs of the human heart, and then on to the promise of grace for pardon, cleansing, and peace—all leading up to the idea of service.

One of the Scripture lessons might be the prophet's vision of the valley full of dead men's bones, very many and very dry.[7] Those dry bones are like many of these details about worship, before they yield to the quickening power of the Holy Spirit. Instead of gathering up the bones and trying to piece them together, the minister

[6] Matt. 17:1-9, 14-21 (A. R. V.). In the Greek, the verb *transfigured* is the same as the dominant verb in Rom. 12:2 and II Cor. 3:18.
[7] Ezek. 37:1-10.

181

ought to ask the Spirit of God to clothe them with flesh, and fill them with life. Then there will be unity, and everything else that should be in the worship of God's House. In other words, no lecturer at Yale, Princeton, or anywhere else, can tell how to plan any hour of worship. Under God, that depends upon the place, the time, the minister, and his controlling purpose.

THE PLAN FOR THE NEXT MORNING SERVICE

The best way to learn how to plan, in general, is to plan carefully, week after week. On Tuesday morning when a minister rises from his knees he should begin to think about his coming adventure in worship; and while he is busy about many things, he should let his plans gradually come to life through the gentle workings of subconscious incubation. Sometime during the week, not too late, he should set apart sufficient time to make his plans in concrete detail, keeping in mind the needs of the people. Even though a minister is able to preach to strangers, he can lead in worship better among his friends. In making his plans, he should keep before him certain faces, perhaps eight or ten, and a different group every week, but never with their knowledge. "How will this hymn (or prayer) meet the heart needs of John Small, Mary Brown, or little Susan Smith?" Here, then, is the shepherd, making ready to lead his flock.

The habit of planning during the week should do away with worry. But there is constant need of foresight. When a man has prepared in faith and is ready to preach about "Christ's Cure for Worry," he should set the example by living without worry, working without hurry, and looking forward without fear. But still he should look forward in faith. It is wise to go into the sanctuary before the organist begins to play the prelude and see that everything is as it should be. The best time to locate the passage in the Scriptures is before any layman has entered. In order to avoid the appearance of haste, delay, or confusion in the leadership of worship, it is wise to prepare the altar as carefully as Elijah did on Mount Carmel. Though the fire to consume the waiting sacrifice must come down from God, he never does for the minister what the minister ought to do for him. Only a man's best is good enough for leading in the public worship of God.

In the hour of worship the minister should set the example of reverent attention to every part of the program. During the sixty minutes between the beginning of the prelude and the pronouncing of the benediction he should never whisper or do anything else that would distract those who are trying to worship. He should enter heartily, though not vociferously, into the singing of every hymn, and listen prayerfully to the special music, both instrumental and vocal, even though the choir may seem to be "rending the anthem." No one but an egotistic boor would go to the Bible and locate his lesson while the choir is singing from Mendelssohn's *Elijah,* "If with all your hearts ye truly seek me, ye shall ever surely find." Equally thoughtless is the practice of poring over

183

sermon notes while everyone else is supposed to be worshiping God.

The best leader does not think about how he is leading. The time for all of those thoughts is past. The finished plans, in so far as they need to be down on paper, are here in the notebook, and that is ever at hand. But better by far is it to have these things in one's mind. If Toscanini can lead his orchestra through any one of a hundred long compositions without once looking at his music, surely the minister of the Gospel should also be able to say what that other artist must feel whenever he lifts his baton for one of those amazing programs which come over the radio: "All things are now ready."

CHAPTER XI

THE IMPORTANCE OF PUBLIC CEREMONIES

A MINISTER'S standing in his own community depends largely upon his ability to lead on special occasions. Such is likely to be the case especially in the country or the small town. Now that there is a radio in almost every home, our people are becoming accustomed to the sort of leadership which does well what it attempts to do; and when their pastor represents them in public, they wish him to make every special service shine. Of course every hour of worship should be as nearly perfect as he can make it; but if once in a while he falls below his high standards, the people will be lenient, unless the lapse comes on a special occasion. In every normal heart there is a strong instinct for the dramatic, and to that God-given tendency such an occasion should make its appeal. As a rule, however, this appeal is indirect. The controlling purpose is to lead in the worship of God. Let us begin with the most difficult of these special occasions.

THE CONDUCT OF A FUNERAL

The funeral service often tests a minister's resourcefulness. Every once in a while the call comes with no warn-

185

ing in advance, and may find the leader unprepared. But if he makes careful preparation whenever there is time, the Lord will take care of him without preparation when there is no such opportunity. The thing to do is to go ahead bravely, by faith. But after such an experience, a minister should see the importance of thinking about such things in general, before he attempts to deal with any one case. Under God, what a man does, or does not, may go far to affect the destiny of the friends who have just been plunged into sorrow.

Many a mature minister has recollections of funerals about which he cares to speak only to God. Before his first experience a certain young pastor had only fifteen minutes in which to shave and change his clothes, with no other time to order his thoughts. In the community he was a stranger, and so the people were curious to know what he would do and say. They were familiar with the facts, as he was not, until afterwards. A little baby, born out of wedlock, had suddenly sickened and died, leaving the father and mother feeling sure that life was not worth what it costs. Fortunately, the minister was wise enough to rely largely upon his book of forms, and in his speaking to stress the fact that death is only a sleep, beyond which the little one awakens in the presence of the Lord Jesus, the Lover of our children.

As a man grows older, if he excels in this part of his work, the calls come more frequently. Occasionally friends expect him to tarry after the death-bed scene and help them lay out the body. In a single day, after lunch, he may have three funerals, each of which calls for a different approach. Sometimes he almost envies the neighboring Roman Catholic priest, who knows exactly what to do in any emergency. But the Protestant way of dealing with each case according to its character is surely better. It would be more nearly ideal if we ministers did as the physicians and surgeons do. In a case which he does not know how to handle, the one in charge consults with a specialist in his field. If there is time, the minister should seek the advice of the brother whose ways of leadership he most highly esteems.

So can the minister learn much from the right sort of undertaker. One night, when a minister's mother was sitting up with the body of the departed, according to a local custom which then prevailed, she asked the undertaker why everything went smoothly at his funerals, but never at those of his competitor. His reply shows the wisdom of inviting such a man to address the ministerial association: "When I am called into a home of sorrow, I learn all the facts; and as soon as I am alone I sit down with pencil and paper to write out in order every step which anyone is to take until the friends come home from the cemetery."

"But do you never have to change your plans?"

"I almost never am able to carry out a service according to my schedule; but if I am ready for ninety and nine details, I do not dread the hundredth. All that I and my helpers have to do is to carry out a service which will call no attention to itself.

187

"If I were a minister of the Gospel, I should be careful in planning for every funeral. In this respect we undertakers notice a great difference among clergymen. When the right sort of man hears the call of sorrow, he goes at once to the home, expresses his sympathy, and does what needs to be done. Unless there is some reason for tarrying, he arranges for a later conference with the widow, or other head of the household; and then he leaves. In a few hours, at the time most convenient to her, the widow should be able to tell him quietly what she and the others in the family circle have decided about the time and the place for the service, the inviting of another minister to take part, and the music, if any. She will not object if the pastor writes down a note here or there, as she has seen the undertaker do. She wishes to be sure that each of them will carry out his part of the service with never a break.

"Without calling attention to the fact, the minister has in mind a series of questions which he asks in making ready for almost every funeral. Is there any passage of Scripture that the friends wish him to read? Do they wish him to read the father's favorite hymn? If there is to be singing, do they wish him to secure persons to do it as volunteers? Do they wish an obituary? If so, he suggests that one of them prepare it, and then he reads it, as from them. Or else he ascertains the facts and writes it out himself. If the father belonged to the Masons, are they to have a part in the service? If so, he suggests that their ritual come first. Then he asks if there is anything

188

else that he and his people can do to help. After such a quiet conversation, closing with a word from the Bible and a brief prayer, the minister should know all that he ought to have in mind as he makes his plans. In the service itself, except in the parts distinctly religious, he remembers that the undertaker is in charge. Each of these two men, in his own special field, wishes to have the sort of service which the friends desire, and which they will always remember with gratitude to God."

The service itself should be simple. If it is held in the home, all that is said and done should call for little more than twenty minutes. In that time, the man who is worthy to lead can say and do a vast deal to bring comfort. If there is singing, as often there should not be, the order of service may be this: a hymn; a psalm or two, such as the one hundred twenty-first, and the twenty-third; a brief prayer, much like an invocation in church, but more tender; a few brief passages from the New Testament, leading up to the first part of John fourteen; the obituary, if any; the remarks, if any; the pastoral prayer, closing with the Lord's Prayer; the closing hymn; and the priestly benediction.

If the minister consulted his own feelings, he would have a still simpler service. There would be no obituary, no music, and no remarks. But in many a parish, such omissions would be unwelcome. In non-essentials it is wise to follow the best local custom. Surely it is possible to have a helpful service either with or without these and other traditional features. When the minister is un-

189

certain whether or not to include a certain feature, in which he personally does not much believe, he is usually wise if he includes it. This is one of the best ways to follow the Golden Rule.

If local custom calls for a sermon, it should be short, yet memorable. Hence one chooses a text which accords with the circumstances, unless they are unpleasant. At the funeral of a farmer one might speak about "The Beginning of the Eternal Harvest." [1] In paying respect to the memory of a good woman, whom the neighbors know as Martha, one might tell how the Lord Jesus loved Martha, as well as Mary and Lazarus; for many people feel that we ministers are not fair to the practical woman, who bears the burdens of the home. When a boy of twelve was electrocuted in the bathroom, the minister spoke briefly from the text, "The streets of the city shall be full of boys and girls playing in the streets thereof." [2] When a girl of five was killed by an automobile while she was playing in the street before her home, the pastor spoke about that golden text, "In my Father's house are many mansions"; that is, there are many rooms in the Father's home.[3] If either minister had used the other one's text, there would have been needless anguish, for one tragedy had occurred in the home and the other in the street. So the pastor should have a heart full of loving sympathy, and a mind stored with the precious promises of the Book.

[1] I Cor. 15:20.   [2] Zech. 8:5.
[3] John 14:2.

Especially in the city, the friends may wish the services to be private. Often that is best. Even so, there should be a definite period of worship, which they will remember as long as they live. Here, as in any other service in the presence of death, the immediate purpose is to bring comfort. That is most likely to come through the careful use of the familiar means of grace, especially the reading of the Scriptures, and the outpouring of the heart in prayer. There is often a place, also, for the right sort of poem; it may be from Browning, Tennyson, or Wordsworth. At the close of the service, when one makes ready to leave, it is good to hand one of the friends a copy of this poem and a list of the Scripture passages, with anything else which will serve as a loving token that the minister shares their sorrow and their hope.

Once in a while there is a funeral service in the church. Then the exercises should be more formal. Though one allows for time in entering the church, and in leaving, one thinks in terms of half an hour. Every such service is likely to have a character all its own. When President Wilson's sister was to be buried beside her father and mother in the churchyard at Columbia, S. C., he sent a messenger from the White House to arrange with the minister for a simple, old-fashioned service, with no sermon. In another parish, when "the flower lady" fell asleep after a long life of radiant usefulness, the services were held at sunset, and the minister spoke from the text, "The beauty of the Lord our God be upon us."[4] Here

[4] Psalm 90:17.

again, the aim is to comfort. A funeral service without comfort would be like a religion without Christ.

At the grave, the time of worship is short. Ordinarily there is a committal service, with little else. If the friends do not care for the committal service, the minister can substitute something like this: a brief psalm, a word of prayer with the Lord's Prayer, a word from the New Testament,[5] the Apostles' Creed, and the covenant benediction. The emphasis is upon the resurrection and the life everlasting. Everyone present is thinking about loved ones whose bodies have been laid to rest, perhaps near by. Hence the call is for words of assurance and hope, rather than lamentations about the cold, clammy clutches of death. In the New Testament, after the Resurrection of our Lord, there is from the lips of a believer scarcely a single note of pessimism and despair. Even at an open grave, therefore, the minister should be the herald of the Good News.

But how can one officiate at the funeral of a scoundrel, who seems to have died in his sins? In such circumstances, one thanks God if one has established the reputation of exalting Christ, and not of appraising the character of the departed. At the funeral of a dear saint of God, if one chooses the lessons with care, and prays in the proper spirit, one can keep away from eulogy, and still make clear how one feels about this departed friend. But in the funeral of a man who is known to have been a sinner, unrepentant, one prefers simply to read the serv-

[5] E.g., Rev. 14:13.

Exalt christ in what he has done.

ice from the denominational book of forms, without any obituary or remarks. What a minister reads out of a standard book seldom gives offence. In the main prayer, it is always proper to beseech the Lord to bless the living, and to use this new experience as a means of grace. At the grave, the committal service should be one that deals with the certainty of death, and the wisdom of making ready for it by getting right with God. This is not the place for the Christian committal service, which speaks of the departed as having gone home to God. The motto is, "Speaking the truth, in love."

THE CEREMONY OF MARRIAGE

The minister who knows how to conduct a funeral is almost sure to know how to officiate at a wedding. In each case, the call is for sympathy, and the use of the imagination. In preaching, and in pastoral contacts, such a man of God exalts the Christian home. He ever shows a tender concern about "the way of a man with a maid." While marriage is not one of our Protestant sacraments, some of us wish that it were. In every way the minister makes it clear that the founding of a new home in Christian love is the most vital experience of life, excepting only that of being born again. If there were more pastoral teaching and preaching about the Christian ideals of marriage, there might be less need for pastoral care of persons who have been divorced.

Every marriage ceremony calls for careful preparation by the clergyman. Hence he has nothing to do with the marriage of those who run away from home, surreptitiously. He does not care to marry strangers. But when one of his friends asks him to officiate at her wedding, he gladly assents, and requests an interview with her and her beloved. When they come to see him, he talks with them about building their new home according to the pattern in the Bible. At least for the first few years of his ministry, he hesitates to talk with such friends about the physical facts of life, preferring to leave all of that to the physician. But the minister stresses the importance of their having a word of grace before every meal, praying together night and morning, and going together to the same church. Before they leave, he learns from the bride, in concrete detail, what sort of ceremony she has pictured in her dreams, and then he helps her put the pieces together. When they rise to go, he asks them to tarry, standing, while he invokes on them the blessing of the Father God.

When the wedding is in the home, the ceremony is simple. Still it should be impressive. Both the bride and the groom should know in advance where they are to stand, what responses they are to make, and how they are to handle the ring, or the rings. If the bride wishes to have music and attendants, there should be a rehearsal, with every person present who is to have a part in the service. As President Francis L. Patton used to say here at the Seminary, "There is nothing extemporaneous about the wedding march, or the bride's gown; and there had better not be anything extemporaneous about the minister's part."

If the service is to be held in the church the minister should prepare still more thoughtfully. The details are likely to differ from those described in the books, but still the pastor and his wife should often refresh their recollection of what every prospective bride reads in Emily Post's *Etiquette*. Otherwise, they may wonder why one of the bridesmaids at the last church wedding sends out of town for a minister who knows how to do everything with a touch of distinction. If local custom permits, such a minister wears his pulpit gown. He uses the stated forms of his church. He may speak these words from his heart, for if he kept holding the book, he might not know what to do with it while handling the ring. Towards the close of the ceremony he comes to the pastoral prayer, which is usually one of his own; and of course he knows it word for word. Thus, in the course of the years, he is the servant of God in founding many a Christian home. Every time he officiates at a marriage, he gets a stronger hold on the hearts of his friends; and he may add to their number, to the glory of his Lord.

THE SACRAMENT OF INFANT BAPTISM

The man with the shepherd heart rejoices when Christian parents bring their baby to the font for baptism. If the father and mother insist, the ceremony may be in their home, or at the Bible school. If so, the minister takes with him one of the officers of the church, and in every way strives to magnify this act of Christian faith. But he prefers to celebrate this holy ordinance as a climactic part of the morning worship, thus affording every member of the church an opportunity to renew his covenant vows. Throughout the year, there should be stated times for infant baptism; it may be on Easter morning, and on the Lord's Day following each communion. However, the parents should feel free to present their babe at any regular service, provided they notify the minister in advance.

If possible, the minister calls in the home during the week before the parents are to present their babe for baptism. Sometimes it is better to have them come to his study. He wishes to help them see the spiritual meaning of this rite, and thus enter into it by faith. He speaks of this beautiful symbol as a sermon in action, showing that this little girl already belongs to God, under the covenant of grace; that she is to be dedicated to a life of service; and that she is to be enrolled as a member of the Visible Church. During this visit, he tries to become well acquainted with the baby, taking her up in his arms if he plans to do so in the service. Otherwise, he might frighten the little stranger. After this interview, which leads up to a brief word of prayer, the minister has on a card the full name of the child and the other facts which should go into the records. Then he arranges with the sexton to put water in the font, and with one of the deacons to meet the parents at the door and remain with them and guide them at every step, if they happen to need guidance.

The ceremony itself, while brief, should be impressive. As a rule, it comes fairly early in the hour of worship—late enough to insure that the parents will be present, and early enough to prevent the little one from growing restless. Since infant baptism calls for one or two prayers, the ceremony may come at the time usually allotted to the pastoral prayer. While the parents are bringing their child to the font, there may be quiet music from the organ, and perhaps gentle singing by the choir. "Shepherd of tender youth" is a blessed old baptismal song. But loud organ music and congregational singing might make the mother and her baby still more nervous. Under the circumstances, it is strange that the little one almost never cries or misbehaves. But if anything of the sort should occur, the minister should remember those strange words of the Psalmist, "Out of the mouth of babes and sucklings hast thou ordained strength."

Here is a service that is somewhat typical. While the parents are bringing their little ones to the font, the officers of the church come forward and take their places on either side of the minister, as the chosen representatives of the people. As at a wedding, the members of the congregation rise and remain standing throughout the ceremony. Except in the last few words of prayer, which are pastoral, the minister follows the established order of his church, perhaps saying these words from memory. After the prayer, the Lord's Prayer, and the priestly benedic-

197

tion, as the parents are leaving the font, the people may join with the choir in singing one or two stanzas of the hymn, "Blest be the tie that binds." The organist keeps on playing the melody until everyone is seated. Meantime, the deacon in charge presents the mother of each child with a little booklet or card containing a copy of the baptismal vows, and a certificate signed by the minister and the clerk of the governing board. On the following Lord's Day, the bulletin gives the names of these little ones whom the Church has openly welcomed to her heart.

THE SACRAMENT OF ADULT BAPTISM

The ceremony of adult baptism should be memorable. Except in a case of sickness or accident, this rite should be solemnized in the church, as a climactic part of public worship. If any candidate wishes to be baptized in secret, the pastor explains to him the meaning of adult baptism as the public confession of faith in Christ. Such an explanation is often necessary, for in some churches many a grown man has never once witnessed this holy rite. In fact, the minister himself, in the denominations which practice infant baptism, may never have seen such a ceremony. If so, he should make an appointment with an older minister and ask him how to make adult baptism as meaningful as it was in the Apostolic Church, and is now in the Cameroun, or the Punjab. Here is the substance of what one young pastor learned from an older minister:—

"The rite of adult baptism ought to be one of the su-

198

preme experiences in the life of the church. When there is to be no celebration of the Lord's Supper, adult baptism comes in the closing minutes of the service. After the sermon, which leads up to the appeal for a personal decision, the minister reads the name of the candidate and asks him to come forward with the officers of the church. When all is ready, the people rise and sing one or two stanzas of the hymn, 'O Jesus, I have promised,' or else, 'O happy day, that fixed my choice.' If the candidate is a woman or a girl the deacon's wife, who is her hostess for the hour, guides her, if necessary, to a place where she can make ready. The ceremony is from the book of forms, with a brief prayer straight from the heart of the pastor. While he and the lay officers are extending the right hand of Christian fellowship, the friends in the choir lead the congregation in singing without announcement another stanza or two of the hymn, 'O let me feel thee near me; the world is ever near.' Then the people all bow down for the benediction, which marks the close of a triumphant hour."

The wise minister is never too old to learn how to lead in such a service more effectively. One way to learn is to visit other congregations. By inquiry among his brethren, he can ascertain when there is to be a baptismal service in the First Baptist Church, or in the Christian Church, at an hour when he is free to attend. While those brethren perform such holy rites in a way which some of us cannot hope to imitate, there is much for any of us to learn. They seem to make adult baptism almost as vital now as it was when Luke wrote the Book of Acts. If the rest of us gave more heed to adult evangelism, we too might have more frequent adult baptisms, and thus begin to recapture the lost radiance of the Christian Church.

THE PUBLIC RECEPTION OF NEW MEMBERS

Such a title is scarcely adequate to show the importance of this public ceremony. Fortunately the book of forms in each denomination tells the minister what he needs to know about the distinctive customs in his own branch of the Church Universal. The main thing, perhaps, is to enter into the preparation imaginatively, and thus to do everything possible to make the ceremony memorable. Otherwise why should there be such a ceremony? Who has not witnessed the ineffectiveness of a service in which there was a mechanical succession of infant baptisms, adult baptisms, the public reception of boys and girls, and the public reception of older people, with nothing to symbolize the momentous meaning of each such holy rite? Sometimes it is proper to bring together the various persons to be welcomed, and to have in the same ceremony various stages, beginning with the boys and girls, and leading up to the welcome of the adults. But there is some advantage in keeping each such ceremony separate, either by having it as the only special feature in the morning hour of worship, or else by having each ceremony at a different period in the hour on some red-letter day, such as Palm Sunday, or Easter. Whatever is worth doing for God in public is worth doing with distinction.

Palm Sunday or Easter morning is a good time to welcome the boys and girls who are putting on the uniform of their King. Throughout the past ten or twelve years, in their homes and in the church, their parents and their pastor, as well as the leaders in the religious work among the children, have been preparing these little ones for the holy hour when they will publicly profess their allegiance to Christ. To this hour many a saintly man should look back when he is old, and tell his grandchildren how he was publicly welcomed into the active membership of the old church back at home. For many of us, alas, there are no such hallowed recollections; for us as boys and girls the admission to the sacred privileges of the church seemed no more meaningful or memorable than any other act of public worship. Hence we understand why the Lutheran and the Reformed Churches magnify the confirmation of baptismal vows.

Whatever the name of the ceremony, it should be vastly more than a passing incident. One way to make it seem vital is for the minister to hold a special class in which he can help the prospective members to prepare for their new privileges and responsibilities. The pastor's class for boys and girls deserves all the praise which it receives. Why should there not also be a class for adults, especially during the weeks before the culmination of the harvest season at Easter? When President Albert W. Beaven, of Colgate-Rochester Seminary, was

201

the pastor of a large Baptist church he seems to have held almost a constant succession of such classes for adults.[6] In the First Presbyterian Church of Neenah, Wisconsin, every man or woman who is to unite with the church, either on confession of faith or by transfer from another congregation, is required to attend the pastor's class for four successive Wednesday evenings. As a consequence, the new members understand what it means to belong to Christ's church, and the congregation as a whole looks upon the public reception of new members as a vital event in the spiritual history of the parish.

In the various denominations the ways of opening the doors of the church to new adult members differ widely. Hence it is not feasible here to enter much into detail. One minister found it good to hold such a ceremony immediately following the morning sermon. While still standing in the pulpit he would read, slowly and solemnly, the names of the members who had died since the last ceremony of the same sort. Then he would read, with equal deliberation and distinctness, the names of those who had been certified to other churches, of those who were coming by certificate from other churches, and of those who were to be received on profession of their faith in Christ. He would ask the congregation to rise and sing the first few stanzas of a familiar hymn, such as "Jesus, I my cross have taken," or else, "Hark, the voice of Jesus calling." During the singing the elders of the

[6] See *The Local Church*, Abingdon, 1937, p. 65; *Putting the Church on a Full-Time Basis*, Harper's, 1930, p. 133; both by Albert W. Beaven.

church would come forward, to stand with him, on either side, facing the people. With the elders would come forward the persons to be welcomed. They would group themselves before the minister; under his leadership they would publicly profess their faith in Christ, and their allegiance to his church. This climactic part of public worship would close with another stanza or two of the same hymn, a word of prayer—to set apart these soldiers of Christ for their service in his name—and the priestly benediction. Then the minister, the elders, and the members of the congregation, coming forward, would extend to the new members the right hand of Christian fellowship.

Here, then, are four different public ceremonies. Instead of being only a passing incident, each of them should be a memorable experience in the lives of God's people, and in the community. In the endeavor to make these ceremonies shine, it would be possible for the pastor to become a sort of ecclesiastical showman; but that is never necessary. It is always proper to appeal to the imagination, provided one does so for the glory of God. The experience of many an honored minister of Christ shows that time and thought devoted to these public ceremonies of the church bring rich dividends for eternity.[7]

[7] Cf. *The Minister in the Modern World,* by R. C. Gillie, A. & C. Black, London, pp. 144-160. Also, *In Pulpit and Parish,* by Nathaniel J. Burton, Macmillan, 1925, pp. 51-87, 139-174.

CHAPTER XII

THE SUPREMACY OF THE LORD'S SUPPER

*T*HE Lord's Supper should be the crowning service in the church, and thus be earth's nearest approach to heaven. Such an experience is like that of the two disciples on the road to Emmaus, though technically speaking, they did not commune.[1] Their hearts burned within them while the Stranger opened to them the Scriptures, and all the more when he made himself known in the breaking of bread. In the holy hour with the Living Christ at his Table, the vital concern is with what he is, and says, and does; not what the leader may be, or say, or do. Of course the leader should be worthy, or he should not be there; but still the healing, cleansing, transforming power of the Lord's Supper depends upon Christ, the Son of God, our Saviour and King, our Divine Helper and Personal Friend. He alone is the Bread of Life.[2]

Such is the teaching of the New Testament. As the hour draws near for the celebration of the Sacrament, the minister should renew his acquaintance with the latter part of each Gospel, and the appropriate parts of First Corinthians.[3] These are the sources of light upon the

---

[1] Luke 24:28-35.   [2] John 6:1-14, 26-66.
[3] Matt. 26:17-30; Mark 14:12-26; Luke 22:7-39; I Cor. 10; I Cor. 11:17-34.

Sacrament. In his teachings from the pulpit, and else-where, he should make so much of this holy ordinance that the people will ask him what it means. At first, the New Testament passages seem disappointing; but on closer view, they suggest ten different ways of looking at the Lord's Supper. According to an interesting book,[4] one of these ways has to do with what is to us the remote past, and one with what we call the unknown future; but all the others have to do with us as believers, here and now. While these ways seem at the start to differ somewhat widely, each of them takes us ere long to the Crucified and Living Lord.

THE MEANING OF THE LORD'S SUPPER

First, here is the memorial of Christ's redeeming grace. "This do in remembrance of me." Like the Passover out of which it grew, the Christian Supper teaches us to look back upon the meaning of our redemption. While the Holy Communion is such a sacred memorial, that should merely be the beginning of our thinking. A mere mem-orialism would be as misleading in one direction as the Roman Catholic Mass is in another. Sometimes we Prot-estants seem to forget that the Lord Jesus, who once died for us and our salvation, is living now, and that he is ever with us, especially at his Table. While we gratefully remember all that he did upon the Cross, we likewise rejoice in all that he is doing now. Though we under-

[4] *The Public Worship of God,* by J. R. P. Slater, Harper's, 1930, pp. 138-174.

stand why our high-church friends twit us about believing in "the real absence," we know that he is with us at his Table, tender to sympathize, and mighty to save.

Second, the Lord's Supper is the symbol of Christ's death for us sinners. "This is my body, which is broken for you." In the Protestant Communion Service, as in the Roman Catholic Mass, everything centers round these words. But we interpret them spiritually, whereas our Catholic friends interpret them literally. Since everything else about the Lord's Supper is symbolic, it would be strange if these words were not. A symbol is a visible sign of some reality which we cannot see. Just as the Cross is the symbol of Christianity, the Lord's Supper is the symbol of what Christ has done and is doing for us through the Cross. When he says, "This is my body," he seems to mean, "This holy sacrament presents to you as believers all the benefits which the Cross makes certain." But the best way to understand such a sacred symbol, with its mystery of light, is to gaze upon it in reverent silence.

Third, the Sacrament is our mightiest means of grace. Grace is the sum of all that we know about God. It is the attraction of his goodness, supremely in the Cross. Grace is the unmerited favor of God to us as sinners. In another sense, it is the power of God, available to us as believers. The means of grace, as we use the term, include the reading of the Bible, private prayer, attendance at public worship, and the Lord's Supper. In each of them, the power comes from God. If grace is divine power for all our needs, then faith must mean human weakness laying hold on divine power, to supply all our needs, through Jesus Christ. At other times of worship the people of God by faith lay hold upon the border of his garment, but at the Lord's Supper they should come face to face with the Living Christ. At those other times there is healing, but here there should be transformation.

Fourth, here is the thanksgiving feast. Such is the literal meaning of that stately title, the Eucharist. In the Greek the original word means thanksgiving. At the Lord's Table we thank him for all his mercies, past, present, and future, as in the one hundred third psalm. Such gratitude centers around the two realities which are most distinctive of Christianity on its human side: the forgiveness of sins and the assurance of the life everlasting. In each of these holy experiences, though the faith is human, the power is divine. That is why we give thanks to God. The more we feel that we are sinners, the more do we rejoice in his salvation. Dear old "Rabbi" Duncan, saintly professor of Hebrew at Edinburgh, said to a humble friend who hesitated to take the cup from his hands because she was a sinner, "Take it, woman, it's *for* sinners."

Fifth, the Eucharist is likewise a family meal. As such, it has among Christians the place which the Passover filled in the religious experience of the ancient Hebrews. The Passover was pre-eminently a family meal. While those people were to give thanks to God for their deliverance as a nation, in the service itself the unit was the family. This seems to have been one of God's ways of

207

teaching those childlike people that the most important place on earth is the home, and that worship ought to be at its best in the family circle. In the New Testament, also, there is much emphasis on the home as the center of life on earth, and on religion as centering in the family, rather than the individual or the nation. The celebration of the Sacrament in the days of the Apostles seems to have been that of one large household coming together to rejoice in God and in each other.

It should still be possible for us to preserve the idea of communing as families, even when we all come together in the House of the Lord. In the olden days, the Scotch custom was to celebrate the Sacrament at a long table, spread with linen spotless white. At each end of the table would stand one of the elders to receive from every communicant a little brass token as a visible symbol of his being a member of the church. At the proper time the members of the congregation would come forward by families. First would be the father, then the mother, and after them the sons and daughters, according to their years. Back in the family pew would be the little boys and girls, doubtless wondering when they too would be counted worthy to take their places with the people of God. Some of these days our younger ministers will perhaps show us how to return to the best in the ways of our fathers. Where it is the custom for the people to come to the altar and kneel down for the Sacrament, there should be no difficulty in leading them to do so by families.

Sixth, this family meal is at the same time the Holy

Communion with the Church of all the ages, on earth, and in glory. That is no small part of what we mean when we stand to say in the Apostles' Creed, 'I believe . . . . in the communion of saints." This word "communion" literally refers to that which we have in common, and surely we who live in the local parish have no monopoly of the Christian faith. Another word which means almost the same as communion is "fellowship." In the original, this word also refers to that which we have in common. The reference, first of all, is to fellowship with the Father and the Son, through the Holy Spirit; but the Beloved Community, which we know as the Church, includes those who are in glory and those who are scattered over the earth. In other words, instead of being provincial, the Christian Church is the most nearly all-inclusive institution which we mortals know.

Here is one of God's ways of leading us out of our excessive individualism. At the Lord's Supper, when our hearts go out to those who are suffering for his sake in lands across the sea, and when we offer thanks for those who are no longer in the flesh, we ought to be lifted up out of our little selves and made to feel something of the spirit of heaven itself. While we know little in detail about heaven and its joys, we know that it is the permanent home of God's redeemed children, and that there they have ideal communion with him and with one another. Perhaps that is why our Lord speaks of heaven in terms of the Communion.[5] There we shall all be one

[5] Matt. 26:29.

united family. When do the members of the family come together more closely than at the table? Of course all of these biblical expressions are figures, but wrapped up in every such figure is a fact of Christian experience or Christion hope.

Seventh, the Holy Communion is likewise the Sacrament. Theologically, the word sacrament means an outward and visible sign of God's inward and spiritual grace. Literally, however, the reference is to the Roman soldier's oath of allegiance to his Emperor. Baptism, also, is a sacrament, in this sense, as in the other. In holy baptism the one who believes in Christ as his personal Saviour publicly accepts him as Lord and Master, and promises to be Christ's loyal soldier until life's very end. In the Lord's Supper from time to time the servant of the Lord renews his vows of loyalty to Christ as the sole Ruler of his heart and life. Especially in explaining the Lord's Supper to young people, we do well to stress this idea of the Sacrament. "The Son of God goes forth to war. . . . . Who follows in his train?"

Eighth, the Sacrament is also a Covenant of Grace. Many of us older folk, whose forbears came from Scotland or the Netherlands, love to think of religion in terms of the Covenant. Sometimes we may push the idea too far, but in its essence it is close to the heart of the Scriptures. When we speak of the Old Testament, or the New Testament, we ought in each case to use the word "Covenant." So ought we to say, "This cup is the New Cov-

enant in my blood," and not, "the New Testament." [6]
In making the Covenant of Grace, the initiative is with
God in Christ. This is the Heavenly Father's way of
pledging to us his redeeming and sustaining grace, so that
by faith we become his people. Here is the foundation of
our Christian faith.

Ninth, there is the sermon in the Supper, the most
powerful and moving sermon in the history of the Church.
In the well-known words of the Apostle Paul, "Ye do
show the Lord's death till he come," the verb translated
"show" literally means, to preach.[7] In the Greek New
Testament this word appears seventeen times, and in all
but two it could be translated "preach," or "proclaim."
In the Supper as the supreme sermon, the subject is the
Lord's death, and the preacher is the congregation. "Ye
do preach." Instead of looking upon themselves as though
they were at a theater, with the minister as the chief actor,
whom they feel free to praise or criticize, the people of
God should come to the Sacrament somewhat as the resi-
dents of Oberammergau come to the Passion Play, in
which they are the actors. Of course someone must lead.
Anton Lang was in charge of the chorus over there in
1930 and 1934, but that humble servant of God was never
in sight when "the Christ" was on the stage. To those
who have the eyes to see it so, the Passion Play is a mighty
sermon about Christ and his Cross.

[6] 1 Cor 11:25.

[7] In the Greek compare the dominant verb in 1 Cor. 11:26 with that in
Acts 4:2 and parallel passages.

In the celebration of the Sacrament how can we set our people free from the balcony attitude, which means that they are watching what they themselves should be doing? Perhaps the best way is to lead in the celebration of the Sacrament so that everyone present will long after the privilege of taking part in preaching this sermon. In a certain church the balconies on either side were usually filled with students from the university and the women's college, some of whom were not professing Christians. Though there was no sermon, or "meditation," before the Supper, the attendance of the students would be as large as at other times, and the interest even greater. After watching the members of the church preach their sermon in action, one or more of those students would come to the officers and ask to be admitted into membership on confession of their faith in Christ. Yes, the Cross still has its ancient power, for it is the Cross of Christ. Never does the Cross appeal more strongly than through this sermon in the Supper.

Tenth, and last of all, the Sacrament is the symbol of Christian hope. When times are hard, and fears abound, this is the aspect which we should stress. Hope! "As often as ye eat this bread, and drink this cup, ye do 'preach' the Lord's death till He come." Here is the one New Testament utterance about the relation between the Lord's Supper and that unknown future which fills many a heart with dire forebodings. Whenever the faint heart is struggling to answer countless unspoken questions about the ways of God in ruling his world, the secret of peace is largely to be found in learning to commit the keeping of all things human into the hands of Christ. While we know not when he is coming, or how, in detail, we know that he will not rest until he wins this old sin-cursed, war-blasted world, which he died to redeem. What a blessed hope!

Here, too, is a message for the person who is thinking more about the sorrows of the past than about the needs of the world tomorrow. There in the pew, feeling all alone, is a widow. She is musing about the husband who once sat by her side, about the little baby who was snatched from her arms when he had scarcely begun to live, and about the son who went out from college to die in distant France. What she needs, again and again, is reassurance concerning the life everlasting, not so much for her own sake as for those whom she still loves more than life. In the Sacrament she learns anew that the Lord Jesus is living now, and that because he lives, they also live with him. And so, with peace in her heart, she returns to her home; and on the morrow she takes up life's burden with new hope, because she has powers more than equal to her tasks. Some day ere long, like Bunyan's pilgrim, she will rejoice to hear the trumpets sounding for her from the other side of the river.

For many reasons, therefore, the Lord's Supper should be the supreme act of Christian worship. The central reason is because he is the Living Christ. Hence we should rejoice, for we assemble with him at his Table, and we do not mourn about him at his tomb. At Jerusalem, in the Church of the Holy Sepulcher, one of our professors learned this truth afresh a few years ago. At five o'clock in the morning, through the kindness of a Dominican monk, this Protestant clergyman was upon his knees, almost within arm's length of that desolate slab where the others were striving by faith to behold the body of the Saviour, as the priest was celebrating the Mass. When those mystic rites were over, the visitor left the place, which seemed to him like a cell, and stumbled out into the open air, murmuring to himself, "They have taken away my Lord, and I know not where they have laid him." But then the minister saw the sun stealing over the Mount of Olives, and his heart began to sing, "When morning gilds the skies, my heart awaking cries, 'May Jesus Christ be praised!'"

Such a transcendent subject as the Lord's Supper deserves a prominent place in a man's sermons. Since the day of the Sacrament affords little opportunity for teaching, a certain wise minister ordinarily deals with the subject on the Sunday preceding. Instead of trying to tell all that he knows about the Sacrament, he takes some one vital truth and then tries to make it shine. For such a purpose, any one of the ten aspects presented above would serve admirably. Again, in appealing to the young people, another minister spoke about "The King's Round Table," with reference to King Arthur. According to that medieval legend, before the king sent his warriors out to befriend the suffering poor, he would call the band together at a round table, where everyone could see the face of the

214

king, as well as the faces of the other knights. So in the Lord's Supper there is the privilege of being with King Jesus, as well as his followers, and of receiving inspiration for arduous service in his name.

THE PREPARATION FOR THE SACRAMENT

While preparation for the Lord's Supper is largely indirect and unconscious, it is good also to prepare directly and consciously. The general principles should emerge while we are thinking about the minister who looks forward to the first Communion in a new parish. Even though the event is to come three months hence, he will find the intervening weeks all too few. Before he tries to lead the people into the holy mount, he should know them, one by one, and love them, as a shepherd knows and loves his sheep. Especially should he know and love, as his brethren in the Lord, the other shepherds of the flock, not thinking of them as "hard-headed business men," or "close-fisted farmers," but as large-hearted men of affairs, who give freely of their time and strength because they love the church. In the first few meetings with the officers, he should encourage them to magnify their calling as the leaders of God's people. If the architecture of the church affords sufficient space, he may invite them to sit with him during the half hour of worship leading up to the Lord's Supper. No minister ever suffers from undue love for his lay brethren. Rather should he rejoice that he need not bear his burdens alone.

In conference with the minister the officers should be

led to prepare for the Sacrament as carefully as the disciples made ready for the Passover on the night before our Lord went out to his Cross. On the evening before Good Friday, at one of our largest congregations in the Middle West, the elders brought in the sacred vessels and spread the holy table after the people had assembled and had sung the Doxology. Evidently the elders had never enjoyed the pastoral leadership of a minister who appreciated the importance of sacred symbols. When intelligent laymen are guilty of such indiscretions, some one of us is usually to blame; for these friends are almost always anxious to do well what they do for the Lord in his House. The wonder is that the wives of the elders did not train them so that they would know enough to set the table before the arrival of invited guests. How much more should everything be ready when people are to be the guests of God!

When a pastor first comes into a field, some of the officers may be on their guard against what seem to them "new-fangled notions." Hence he makes no suggestions, and offers no criticisms, but quietly bides his time. Doubtless because the local leaders feel strongly about the Communion, many a bitter congregational quarrel has arisen over something relating to the Sacrament. At the first celebration, the minister is careful to make his own part as helpful and beautiful as the circumstances permit. If he is approachable, one of the younger officers is likely to come to him afterwards and ask how they can make their part in the celebration more beautiful and impressive.

The minister should thank him for coming, and ask him to bring the matter before the officers. If the way be clear, they should appoint him to confer with the pastor in preparing plans for adoption at the next meeting.

As an object lesson, showing the results of such team-work, there hangs in the study of the First Presbyterian Church, Lexington, Va., a neat diagram of the pews and aisles, showing each officer where he is to stand, as well as how he is to move. In another church where the arrangement of the pews is complicated, on the Sunday before the Sacrament each officer receives from the layman in charge a mimeographed sheet of suggestions telling him exactly what he is to do. In each of those congregations the Lord's Supper seems to have become the most notable event in the services of the church. Since each congregation ministers to students, who will later go back to their home churches and in time perhaps become church officers, it is fitting that these young people should see the wisdom of doing all things decently and in order. But there is need of a quiet reform in many congregations without any student constituency.

The minister should also confer with the organist and the leader of the choir, so that there will be mutual understanding. Since it is easier for one man to conform with local custom than for the people to change the habits of years, the new minister plans to do what his predecessors have done, in so far as he can with a clear conscience. For example, in a church where the communicants receive the elements in the pews, during the distribution of the

217

bread there may be silence, since many a heart is busy with memories of loved ones no longer in the flesh. But during the distribution of the wine there may be gentle music, partly because there is likely to be confusion in the handling of the cups. If there is music, it may be simply the organ melodies of rich old hymns about the Cross, or else the choir may sing them softly. At the close of the service, the organist may lead up to the final hymn of triumph, such as "Crown him with many crowns," or "All hail the power of Jesus' name," or the "Gloria in excelsis."

Much more vital is the preparation in the hearts of the people. In the Sacrament there is naught of magic. Hence careless communicants may fail to receive what it has to give. Here is a fruitful subject for conversation and prayer in many a pastoral call. More direct, as well as more satisfactory, is the teaching in the pastor's class, whether for adults or boys and girls. One whole session may have to do with the Lord's Supper. Like Henry van Dyke when he was a lad, one or two members of the class may be afraid to commune. Usually the reason is because of that verse which the King James translates incorrectly, "He that eateth and drinketh unworthily, eateth and drinketh damnation to himself, not discerning the Lord's body." [8] This is simply a warning against coming to the Communion without seeing in it the symbol of Christ's Cross. The word "damnation" ought rather to be "judgment," as it is in the American Revised Version. Here,

[8] I Cor. 11:29.

218

then, is an opportunity for a popular exegesis of a passage which is seldom understood.

A still more direct way to prepare for the Sacrament, especially among adults, is to hold preparatory services. Often they begin on the preceding Sunday, and include the evenings of Wednesday, Thursday, and Friday, but not Saturday. A still better plan, where feasible, would be to have simultaneous cottage prayer meetings in various districts of the parish, on Monday and on Friday evening, for a week or two, and then to hold the preparatory services. In any case, one does not judge the meetings primarily on the basis of the number who attend, but rather by the effectiveness of the preparation for the Sacrament.

Whatever the plan, it should become a part of the parish traditions. A fairly good plan, followed for several years, would be better than many brilliant experiments, each carried out once. Only by repetition will such a way of serving God find its place into the religious habits of a people. In the First Presbyterian Church of Wilmington, N. C., ever since the pastorate of Joseph R. Wilson, the people have assembled at the church each morning except Saturday during the week before the May Communion. To those meetings "Tommy" Wilson, as Woodrow then was called, must have gone as a lad. At present the plan is to gather at eight o'clock and enjoy twenty minutes of inspiring worship, so that the boys and girls may go to school with the fathers on their way to work. The attendance is so large that the meetings must be held in the main sanctuary. Partly for this reason, the May

Communion is the religious event about which those good people tell their winter guests from the North. So in every parish the wise minister plans with his officers according to local conditions and needs.

THE CELEBRATION OF THE SACRAMENT

Opinions differ concerning the wisdom of celebrating the Sacrament frequently. On one hand, some of the fathers in the Highlands of Scotland used to have Communion only once a year. On the other hand, Calvin wished to have it every Lord's Day, as the friends do in the Church of Christ today. In any case, the minister conforms largely with the best traditions of his denomination, and his present parish. Perhaps the two extremes meet best when there is such a celebration once a month, alternating between the morning and the evening service. That is the plan in the Fourth Presbyterian Church of Chicago, though they have Communion, also, at certain special seasons. Of course such a plan is most successful in a large congregation, with an evening constituency somewhat different from that in the morning. Communion at night is peculiarly impressive.

Opinions differ, too, about the wisdom of holding the Communion on Easter. Many of us prefer the evening before Good Friday, or else at the close of a three-hour afternoon service on Good Friday itself. Another time of rare beauty is on the evening of Easter Day, as the sun is setting, for that seems to have been the hour when the Lord Jesus made himself known in the breaking of bread.

220

At the morning service on Easter there are almost always many visitors, some of whom worship in public regularly once a year. While they are welcome, they surely are not ready to commune. Is it not better to have the Communion at some other time, and thus let Easter shine in its own blessed light? As for the hour, custom suggests that the Communion comes most fitly, as a rule, where the Roman Catholics often put the Mass, at the time when the sun is almost at the zenith. When shall we learn to think of religion in terms of light?

In the service itself, whatever the time, the approach to the Sacrament should be gradual. The earlier parts of worship should be shorter than on other days, so that the people will not feel worn out before the time to commune. Since the sacramental service itself provides for something equivalent, it should be possible to omit one of the early hymns, the responsive reading, and the longest of the prayers. If there is a sermon, or a pastoral "meditation," it should be short and simple, yet exquisite in its way, since it has been on the minister's heart for long. For his text he may often turn to the mountain country in the Gospel of John, beginning at the thirteenth chapter; and if the architecture is of a certain type, he may speak much about the Upper Room. In any case, the appeal is to the heart.

But many a minister who greatly believes in preaching wonders why he should have a sermon on the high day of the Sacrament. He knows that in the Reformation the sermon took the place which the Roman Catholics had

given to the Mass. Since the Lord's Supper too is a sermon, a sermon in action, is not this message more likely
to find its way to the heart if there is no other message
during the same hour of worship? At any rate, the most
vivid memories that some of us cherish concerning the
Sacrament are of hours when there was no spoken sermon
or meditation. However, this is another good place for
the minister to show his humility by deferring to the best
local custom, without seeming to be making any sacrifice.
It is possible to have a blessed sacramental service either
with or without a sermon. A sermon is a sort of sacrament in speech, and a sacrament is surely a sermon in
symbol. In any parish, the people worship best in the way
in which they have worshiped most profitably at other
times.

In any case, the sacramental service should glow with
a light as from above. Hence the minister does well to
have in his heart, and often to say to himself in private,
the exact words of the service in his own denominational
book. He should know exactly where each holy vessel
is to rest on the table, and when the officers are to remove
the cloth. In handling the trays for the individual communion cups he should know how to avoid noise and
confusion. He should take hold of each plate or tray
with both hands, holding it all the while on the level. He
should school himself to move and speak slowly. Although there is nothing magical about the bread and the
wine, he should be careful not to spill a crumb or a drop
upon the carpet or the linen. In other words, without

calling attention to the fact, he should be complete master of the situation. That calls for the constant use of the imagination.

Under God, the value of the Sacrament depends largely upon its symbolism. Sometimes the people are more sensitive about symbolism than the minister seems to be. So they feel starved in this part of their nature. They feel that though their minister can preach with power he is too brisk, too direct, too commonplace, in his ministry at the Lord's Table. Sometimes they wonder whether or not he has prepared for such handling of holy things. They feel that the hour brings them nothing of heaven on earth, nothing like the experience of the mountain top, with its air of greater visibility into the mysteries of God and eternity. For example, when he takes upon his lips the holy words of his Lord—"Drink ye all of it"—he makes this saying about the unity of God's household sound as though it were an injuction to consume all of the wine. The mastery of such details, however, belongs in the study, and in the place of secret prayer. When the leader stands at the Table of the Lord, let him think about the things which matter most for time and eternity.

Is it any wonder that the holiest man of God shrinks from standing in such a glare of light? Never do his own sins and shortcomings seem so ghastly, so that he fears lest they come between the people and their Lord. What if his touch should soil the vessels of mercy and thus prevent the waiting people from receiving God's blessing?

When such feelings rush into a man's soul and threaten to interfere with his leadership, all that he needs to do is to commit himself anew into the hands of his Lord, and then go on, in faith. While that may not be easy, it should always be possible, by grace. If he wishes his friends to think about Christ, let him also think about Christ. Above all, when the service reaches its climax, and he pauses in the midst of his prayer to invoke the blessing of the Holy Spirit upon the bread and wine, he and the people alike should feel that the heavens are open, and that the glory of God is shining in the face of Jesus Christ.

Such a minister longs to share the joys of the Sacrament with those who cannot be present. So the bulletin announces that in the afternoon, where the members of the family so desire, he and one of the lay officers will call upon the sick and the infirm to administer the Communion. In such a mission the layman carries a private communion set, and at each upper room he spreads the table. The service is brief, partly because the strain might otherwise be too much for the one who is frail, and likewise because the minister still has much to do that day. But he should never seem to be in haste. As soon as the service is ended, he and his helper steal out of the room quietly, perhaps leaving the aged grandmother sitting by the western window, where she will wait for the sun to go down, as a symbol that for her, ere long, there will be a family reunion in the Father's Home. That night, as she says her prayers, she will thank God that the dominie and the others in the kirk are never too busy to think about her as a daughter of the King.

After such a day, even the most stalwart man of God feels weary—as George Whitefield once said, at the end of an exhausting day, "Lord Jesus, I am weary in thy work, but not of it." Once in the sanctuary, or perhaps twice, and then in a succession of homes, the minister has led the people of God into the mount; and with them he has looked upon the face of the King. While he has gone through each service in faith, still he is human; and after it all is over, there may be a reaction. But if he has done the will of God as the leader of his people, the minister should commit them to the care of the One who never slumbers or sleeps, and then lie down to rest, assured that all is well with his friends, both now and forevermore.[9]

[9] Cf. *Reality in Worship*, by Willard L. Sperry, Macmillan, 1926, pp. 178-188.

CHAPTER XIII

THE TRAINING OF THE LEADER IN WORSHIP

THE man who leads in the public worship of God should know how. In a sense this rare sort of ability comes from God as a gift; but in another sense the art of leadership is the result of long and careful training, in which every man has to be largely his own teacher. If he were a Roman Catholic, with forms of worship highly standardized, he might master his technique while still in the seminary; but if he belongs to a Protestant church, which expects him to deal with each situation according to its character, he must keep on learning as long as he lives. This is one of many reasons why the work of the ministry lays a mighty hold upon a good man's heart. Worship is adventure.

The man who leads well in various sorts of public worship is an artist second to none. An artist is one who conforms with certain laws in order to attain certain ends. Before the leader in worship can conform with the laws of his art, he must know these laws, and then he must keep on using them until it becomes almost a matter of second nature to do his work as it should be done. Just as the sculptor should know human anatomy, or the architect the principles of engineering, and then learn how to use this knowledge in creative endeavor, so must the leader in worship toil in mastering his laws, and in learning to use them well.[1]

Like every other artist, the leader in worship should be a master of his craft. His craftsmanship is an index to his character. But such leadership calls for something far higher than craftsmanship. The man who learns from books, and from men, how to lead in worship, and then simply carries out these rules, is only an artisan. The difference between the artist and the artisan is that the one uses such means for the glory of God, and in his own way; the other seems to use them for their own sake, and sometimes he is a slave to his system. While these distinctions are seldom so absolute in practical experience as they seem to appear on paper, they bring out the fact that leadership in the worship of God calls for something far higher than mechanical obedience to rules. When a semi-mechanical minister tries to lead in public worship, a little boy may whisper to his mother, as he did when he first saw the body of a dead man, "Mother, is he real?"

The minister who wishes to master this finest of the fine arts should form regular habits of study. As in preparing to preach, there is a subtle temptation to wait for some sort of inspiration, which often proves to be desperation, and then plan for public worship. But that is not the way the real artist works. Here is part of an interview with Thomas Mann, winner of the Nobel Prize in literature:

[1] Cf. *In a Day of Social Rebuilding*, by Henry S. Coffin, Yale Press, 1918, pp. 82-108.

"I make it a rule to devote all of my mornings to my novel. I usually get to work at half past eight and write until about twelve-thirty. I don't wait for inspiration, for I have discovered that if one waits for it one is sure to be disappointed. Writing is a habit which if cultivated will grow." [2] In this connection he tells about his next novel, and then about the one after that—another in the series about Joseph. What an example for the busy pastor in his daily study!

THE STUDY OF SACRED BOOKS

As in learning how to preach, the best place to begin any course of home study about worship is with the Bible. Here the minister should saturate his soul in the most beautiful parts, such as the Psalms, and the most moving passages written by the prophets. Since the hour of worship should be notable for its gentle rhythm, most of it in prose, he may well commit to heart a number of the parables in Saint Luke, as well as other passages like the ones listed below. For instance, the thirteenth chapter of First Corinthians is perhaps the most exquisite piece of rhythmical prose in the English New Testament. Far more vital, however, than their literary charm is the transforming influence which streams from these golden chapters. The passages which are most inspiring as literature are most helpful in leading the minister close to the heart of God. This particular list represents the favorite chapters of the people in two different parishes, and of students

[2] *New York Times Magazine*, Oct. 23, 1938, p. 22.

in two different seminaries. In three or four of the passages, the chapter divisions in our English Bible do not correspond with the units of thought and feeling; so each minister should make a list of his own.

Genesis 1	Matt. 5-7	Acts 2
Exodus 20	Luke 2	Romans 8 (or 12)
Psalm 23	Luke 15	I Cor. 13
Psalm 103	Luke 24	I Cor. 15
Psalm 121	John 1	II Cor. 5
Isaiah 40	John 10	Phil. 4
Isaiah 53	John 14	Heb. 11
Isaiah 55	John 15	Rev. 21

Invaluable, also, is the hymnal, much of which the minister should know by heart. While he may not quote often from hymns, at least not in his prayers, he should be able to sing many a song of the Church without glancing at the book. If the people love their pastor, they will soon learn to love the books which he loves best; and that may mean, in this order, the Bible, the hymnal, and the lives of the missionaries—but that is another story.

Likewise should one spend much time among the books of devotion, committing to memory parts of these masterpieces, and thus learning how to share the spirit of Augustine, or of Bunyan. The aim is not to be able to quote, or even to echo, but to climb with the saint of God to the mountain top of Christian experience, and thus commune with The Eternal. Here is Christian mysticism at its best; at its best it keeps close to the Living Christ as he makes himself known in the Scriptures. Hence any one of the books listed below would be a worthy gift from the mistress of the manse to her beloved when he is being slapped on the back and told that he is "a live wire." In the midst of countless temptations to make his ministerial life a sort of merry-go-round, let him often turn to the devotional classics, written by men who knew how to pray as well as how to write. Through one's denominational bookstore, one can purchase these books at a moderate cost.[3]

The direct result of such reading ought to be the deepening and enriching of a man's spiritual life. As one of the by-products, there is almost certain to be more of beauty and persuasiveness in his spoken words, especially when he prays. There is a language of devotion which differs from the speech of the street much as the heavens differ from the earth. While the man in the pew uses this latter sort of speech from day to day, he enjoys something different when his minister leads in public prayer. Then, if ever, one should be able to lift up one's eyes to the hills and use words which have about them little that is of the earth, earthy. On the other hand, such diction quickly becomes forced, and then it seems unreal. But if the man of God saturates his spirit in the devotional classics, he can trust his heart to have its way, whenever he leads the people to the mercy seat. Here are some of the devotional classics:

Augustine, Bishop of Hippo: *Confessions*

[3] See *A Library of Religion,* by Anthony C. Deane, London, 1918.

Andrewes, Bp. Lancelot: *Manual of Private Devotions*
Bunyan, John: *Pilgrim's Progress* and *Grace Abounding*
Baxter, Richard: *Saint's Everlasting Rest*
Herbert, George: *Country Parson*
Rutherford, Samuel: *Letters*
Taylor, Bishop Jeremy: *Holy Living* and *Holy Dying*
Phelps, Austin: *The Still Hour*

THE USE OF SPARE TIME

Since public worship is a fine art, the minister can prepare for leadership, indirectly, and perhaps unconsciously, by learning to love and enjoy such fine arts as poetry and the drama, music and painting, as well as architecture. Each of these in its own way ministers to the love of beauty, and likewise appeals to the imagination. Thus the growing familiarity with the masterpieces in any of these arts tends to keep the minister from becoming coldly intellectual, or prosaically commonplace. While he should be reasonably familiar with all of these arts, he will probably wish to make some one of them a sort of intellectual hobby. For instance, J. V. Moldenhawer of the First Presbyterian Church in New York seems to live largely among the English poets, both classic and contemporary.

Christian worship is closer akin to poetry than to almost anything else outside the Church. That is why some of us feel that the chief defect in the education of the present-day minister is likely to be in his lack of love for the best in his own literature. According to Frederick W.

231

Robertson, who is "the preacher's preacher," one can judge a clergyman fairly well when one knows which poet he loves best. In his sermon a man may glibly refer to Milton and Dante, or Francis Thompson and Alfred Noyes, and perhaps repeat excerpts from Bartlett's *Familiar Quotations,* or Burton Stevenson's books; but does the man who quotes really know any one of these guides into the mystic realm of beauty as a man knows his dearest friend? If so, the lover of true poetry is almost certain to be able to use in public worship the sort of words which are worthy of their calling.

Another hobby which is rewarding is the study of paintings. One who dwells near a large city can spend many a happy Monday afternoon with his wife in the museum of fine arts, listening to the lecture about the paintings of Velasquez, or the thirteenth century tapestries, and then looking at the creations themselves to see the beauty which has hitherto been hidden. If the minister dwells far from the city, he and his wife can arrange to spend a part of their midsummer holiday in Chicago near the Field Museum, or in New York, near the Metropolitan. In either city, they can enjoy fine art by day, "without money and without price," as well as wonderful music by night, at a cost which almost any purse can afford. During the preceding winter they can read about what they hope to see; and perhaps they will dream about going to the National Gallery in London, or Pitti Palace in Florence. Such visions may never come true, but it costs nothing to build castles in the sky, and they are safer by far than castles in Spain. Somehow or other, the man who wishes to lead in worship should keep his ideals shining.

The one diversion which is most certain to help many a minister is music. Now that the radio has come into almost every manse, the rarest of music can be heard almost every night. As William Lyon Phelps of Yale assures us out of his rich personal experience, almost any intelligent person of mature years can learn to enjoy the music of Beethoven and Brahms, or even that of Bach and Wagner. The man who follows the *Ninth Symphony* of Beethoven, as rendered by the musicians under Toscanini, or *The Passion of our Lord, according to Saint Matthew,* the work of Bach, as rendered by the Boston Symphony Orchestra under Koussevitzky, is saturating his soul in heavenly beauty. Even better is it to play for oneself upon the violin or the piano, and to sing the melodies which the musical world shall never cease to love.

Still another hobby should call for the open-air treatment of the soul. One may work in the garden, first planning it as a whole, much as one plans for the work of the Christian year; and then one can think about each separate bed, much as one prepares for a single Sunday service. Thus through the summer one can hope to have a constant succession of beauty and helpfulness, for one will share the fruits of such early morning toil.

During the winter, one can walk. It may be out over hills in the country, or else through crowded streets in the city. One ought ever to be watching for beauty.

Otherwise, one's ways of speech in the hour of worship may sound like the product of dreary cogitations over musty books, and not like the outpouring of a heart which is in love with everything beautiful.

But where can one find the time for these exacting ways of preparing, indirectly, to lead in worship? The obvious reply is that some ministers do such things, and that no one of them has more than twenty-four hours in the day. The idea is to budget one's time, and then to live according to some schedule, which must be elastic. How otherwise could such New York pastors as Ralph W. Sockman, Paul E. Scherer, and George A. Buttrick keep up with their manifold labors and still make frequent excursions into the realms where beauty dwells? The same is true of many a minister about whom the world never hears, for the metropolitan centers have no monopoly of the men who know how to lead in public worship.

THE DISCIPLINE OF THE SOUL

Whenever a man excels in this holy art, it is safe to surmise that he has known the discipline of pain. In North Carolina, the pastor of a fairly large rural church lay on his bed throughout an entire summer, slowly recovering from typhoid fever. On each Lord's Day, the people assembled for Bible study and prayer, but there was no minister, and there was no preaching. In the autumn when the pastor returned to his pulpit he found that the spiritual life of the people was on a higher plane than it had ever been. The reason, doubtless, was because of intercessory prayer. While they had been praying for him, he had been praying for them. Every twenty-four hours that summer, beginning each day at a different place, that man of God would talk with his Heavenly Father about the soul of every man, woman, or child, white or black, Christian or not, within five or six miles of that church.

The radiance of such a man's life keeps on shining long after he himself has gone home to his God. That man's son is now in the ministry, and doubtless the people who learned to love the father all the more because they kept praying for him are now asking God to let his mantle fall upon the son, with a double portion of the same spirit—the mantle of service and the spirit of prayer. This is the true apostolic succession.

In the history of the Church, many a man has learned how to lead others to the throne of God by sitting at the feet of an older minister who has come to know Him in some fiery furnace. This is the sort of minister who should lead the morning devotions at the annual meetings of the conference or the synod. The effect is more likely to be lasting if the same man leads from day to day. The purpose of each hour is to lead in prayer and in praise, with readings from the Book, not to entertain or even to instruct. After such daily meetings with the Lord and his chosen leader, many a minister should go down to his home, as his father used to come away from the hour of worship under John Henry Jowett, resolving,

235

"By God's grace I, too, shall learn to lead in public worship, especially in prayer."

The best way to learn how to lead in public worship is to pray in the closet. That may mean a certain place in the study, or else in the home, where one's soul can be insulated from the world, and be in vital touch with God. More often the "live-wire parson" is in close touch with the telephone, and is almost wholly insulated from God. Hence he is likely to be popular with worldly men. But his brisk, business-like air does not prove uplifting when he leads in worship. On the other hand, the minister who prays much in private is eager to pray with his people, either in their homes or when they come to see him, one at a time, in his study. In this latter way, John Sutherland Bonnell is rendering a unique and far-reaching service at the Fifth Avenue Church in New York.[4] So is Harry Emerson Fosdick at the Riverside Church. Any such skillful ministry with the individual is certain to react favorably upon all that the minister does in the hour of worship.

Such a physician of the soul is Leslie D. Weatherhead, the Wesleyan clergyman who has become the pastor of the Congregationalists at the City Temple in London. He is perhaps the most popular preacher in England today. In a recent message to his brother ministers he calls for "a radiant, vivid, transforming, communicable experience of Christ." In the same connection he says, "I found it a good plan on a Saturday evening to go into

[4] Cf. *Pastoral Psychiatry*, by John S. Bonnell, Harper's, 1938.

the City Temple and sit in the place where the people in difficulty come to worship, and try to get right inside their personalities and pray for them. . . . It is a bargain that when they come to church next Sunday, I, who have been set aside and allowed to climb the heights, shall have something to say to them about the dawn." [5]

Thus we have been thinking about the preparation which is indirect, and often unconscious. Even when the minister goes into the sanctuary on a Saturday evening and moves about among the pews, praying by name for one friend after another, the burden on the heart is not that of the service on the morrow. The idea is rather that the prepared minister is better than the prepared service, and that the best preparation of one's heart for leading others in prayer when they are present is to pray for them when they are absent. But the minister who thus crowns each busy week with definite prayers for his people is the very one who is most sure to prepare for his public leadership in ways both conscious and direct.

Since we have been thinking about such ways of preparation as we have considered the hymns, the readings from the Bible, and the prayers, as well as the entire service, we need not cover that ground again, even in review. The main thing is for each man to determine how he can do this work most effectively, and then set apart a definite period every week, perhaps an entire forenoon. Anyone who will do this every week for five or ten years

[5] *The Message and Method of the New Evangelism,* edited by Jesse M. Rader, Round Table Press, 1938, p. 28.

will have gained a mastery of this fine art, but not a perfect mastery, for that will never come on earth.

From day to day, let the man ordained of God to lead in public worship dedicate himself anew to his high calling: "Here am I, O Lord, an earthen vessel. Take me just as I am, cleanse me by thy Holy Spirit, and fill me with thy blessed Word. Then shall I lead in the worship of thy House so that the people will lose sight of me, because every eye will be fixed on the Lord Jesus."

"It were to be wished the flaws were fewer
In the earthen vessel, holding treasure. . . .
But the main thing is, does it hold good measure?
Heaven soon sets right all other matters." [6]

[6] Robert Browning, "Christmas Eve," canto xxii.

THE LITERATURE OF THE SUBJECT

*I*N the field of history the best-known book is probably *Christian Worship,* by L. Duchesne, translated by M. L. McClure, S.P.C.K., London, 1919. Much more practical is *A History of Christian Worship,* by Oscar Hardman, Cokesbury, 1937. The best-known books about theory include *Reality in Worship,* by Dean Willard L. Sperry, of Harvard, Macmillan, 1926; *Worship,* by Evelyn Underhill, Nisbet and Co., London, 1936; and *The Spirit of Worship,* by Friedrich Heiler, Hodder & Stoughton, London, 1926. *Le Culte,* in three volumes, by Robert Will, Paris, 1925-35, ought to be translated, at least in part. *The Idea of the Holy,* by Rudolf Otto, translated by J. W. Harvey, Oxford, 1923; and *The Religious Consciousness,* by James B. Pratt, Macmillan, 1928, deserve careful study.

The practical books include *The Public Worship of God,* by J. R. P. Sclater, Harper's, 1930; *The Technique of Public Worship,* by J. H. Odgers and E. G. Schutz, Methodist Book Concern, 1928; *The Quest for Experience in Worship,* by Edwin H. Byington, Harper's, 1929; and *The Recovery of Worship,* by George W. Fiske, Macmillan, 1931. The better books about church music include

The History and Use of Hymns and Hymn Tunes, by David R. Breed, Revell, 1934; *Lyric Religion,* by H. Augustine Smith, London, 1931; and *The Hymnody of the Christian Church,* Stone Lectures, by Louis F. Benson, Doran, 1927. The most valuable work here is the book issued by a man's own denomination, such as *Our Hymnody,* by Robert G. McCutchan, Methodist Book Concern, 1937; or the *Handbook to the Hymnal,* by William C. Covert and C. W. Laufer, Presbyterian Board, 1935.

The best-known book about prayer is probably *Das Gebet,* by F. Heiler; but the translation by Samuel McComb, *Prayer,* Oxford Press, 1932, omits some of the most helpful parts. *The Prayers of the Bible,* by John E. McFadyen, London, 1906; and *Extempore Prayer,* by Marshall P. Talling, Manchester, 1902, are to be had only second-hand; each is worthy of a reprint. *The Catholic Book of Prayers* costs a dime, at Woolworth's; and the Protestant Episcopal *Book of Common Prayer* is inexpensive, as well as invaluable. *Prayers for Services,* by Morgan P. Noyes, Scribner's, 1934, includes a bibliography. *A Book of Invocations,* by Herman P. Guhse, Revell, 1928; and *Let Us Worship God,* by Hubert L. Simpson, London, n. d., are suggestive.

Most practical are *The Cokesbury Funeral Manual,* 1932, and *The Cokesbury Marriage Manual,* 1933 (revised 1939), both edited by William H. Leach. *Training Young People in Worship,* by E. L. Shaver and H. T. Stock, Pilgrim Press, 1929, is a textbook approved by the

240

International Council of Religious Education. *The Bond of Honour,* by B. S. Easton and H. C. Robbins, Macmillan, 1938, contains a brief bibliography about the minister's relation to marriage. *Why Worship?* by Muriel Lester, Cokesbury, 1937, a booklet costing twenty-five cents, should be helpful in arousing lay interest.

After poring over all these books, and many others, one feels that the best way to learn to lead in worship is to use the Bible and the hymnal, with frequent reference to such a work as *The History of the Christian Church,* Philip Schaff, in seven volumes, Scribner's, 1890, all the while seeking the guidance of the Holy Spirit, as one learns to do by doing. "If any man willeth to do his will, he shall know of the teaching." [1]

[1] John 7:17*a*.

INDEX

243

INDEX

Jowett, John H., 25, 166-67
Junior sermon, 157

Kelman, John, 103, 176
Kirk, Harris E., 60

Laws of Habit, 77-80; of Learning, 122-24
Lay officers, 168, 197, 203, 215-17
Leadership of worship, 13-30, 226-38; difficulty of, 23-25; necessity of, 20-23; personality of leader, 25-29; training for, 226-38
Learning, Laws of, 122-24
Lectionary, 137-41
Lexington, Va., 217
Literature of worship, 239-41
Liturgy, 51-73; argument for, 61-66; argument against, 66-70; meaning, 61; optional liturgy, 71-73
Liverpool, England, 82, 156
Lord's Prayer, 66, 150, 160
Lord's Supper, 204-25; celebration, 221; Christian comfort, 212-13; Easter Communion, 216, 220-21; effect on child, 88-89; frequency, 46, 220; music, 217-18; night, at, 220; preaching at, 211, 214, 221-22; preparation of officers, 215-17; preparation by pastor, 215; preparatory services, 218-20; shut-ins, for, 224; symbolism, 93, 223-24; ten aspects, 205-15
Loyalty, 87-88
Luther, Martin, 55-58, 117
Lutheran churches, 56, 64, 112, 201

McAfee, Cleland B., 136-37
McCosh, James, 165
McFadyen, John E., 171
Mackay, John A., 68, 152

Maclaren, Alexander, 170
Malachi, 37
Mann, Thomas, 228
Marriage ceremony, 57, 157, 193-95
Martha and Mary, 13, 134, 190
Mason, Lowell, 116, 118
Matheson, George, 113
Melody, 116, 118
Members, reception of, 200-03
Mendelssohn-Bartholdy, Felix, 183
Merrill, William P., 98, 125
Messiah, The, 29-30, 92, 115
Methodist: churches, 57-58, 107; Hymnal, 101-02, 109
Micah, 21
Michelangelo, 28, 55, 65
Middle Ages, 52-54
Missions, 43, 45, 49, 198
Moldenhawer, J. V., 231
Music: anthems, 19, 85, 96, 126, 176; choir, 35-36, 95, 98, 121, 176; committee, 97, 107, 132; congregational singing, 96, 109, 115, 124; minister's knowledge of, 98-103; money for, 35, 42, 97-98, 107; organist, 96, 98-99, 126, 130, 197, 217; pastor's relation to, 95-98, 107; prelude, 91-92, 96, 144, 176; processional, 36, 97; responses, 96; solo, 96; training the people, 96-98; see also Hymns, Hymn tunes

Neenah, Wis., 202
New Testament worship, 39-49, 66

Old Testament worship, 31-39
Older people, 100-02, 121
Organist, 96, 98-99, 126, 130, 197, 217

Parker, Joseph, 149
Passion Play, 53, 211
Pastor's class, 121, 132, 201-02, 218

245

INDEX